# Seeds *of* Courage

---

# Seeds *of* Courage

Stories, ideas and snippets of wisdom on
how to live a big life through small
and gentle acts of courage

## VARI McKECHNIE

Copyright © Vari McKechnie 2023
First published by the kind press, 2023

The moral right of the author to be identified as the author
of this work has been asserted.

All rights reserved. Without limiting the rights under copyright reserved above, no part of this publication may be reproduced, stored in or introduced into a retrieval system, or transmitted, in any form or by any means (electronic, mechanical, photocopying, recording or otherwise) without the prior written permission of the publisher of this book.

A catalogue record for this book is available from the National Library of Australia.

Trade Paperback ISBN: 978-0-6455978-0-6
Hardback ISBN: 978-0-6455978-4-4
eBook ISBN: 978-0-6455978-1-3

Cover and internal design by Vari McKechnie
Author photograph by EJ Hassan

Print information available on the last page.

The kind press acknowledges Australia's First Nations peoples
as the traditional owners and custodians of this country,
and we pay our respects to their elders, past and present.

www.thekindpress.com

While the publisher and author have used their best efforts in preparing this book, the material in this book is of the nature of general comment only. It is sold with the understanding that the author and publisher are not engaged in rendering advice or any other kind of personal or professional service in the book. In the event that you use any of the information in this book for yourself, the author and the publisher assume no responsibility for your actions.

*To Dad, thank you for passing on your love of books to me. I miss you. Although I know you're still here with me in many ways, I wish I could call you and say, 'Look! I did it! I wrote a book!'*

# Contents

Why we need courage before bravery     1
Introduction     5
How to use this book     9

## Part 1 Tilling The Soil     13

Start     17
Safety enables risk     19
Joyful discomfort     21
You are the narrator     23
Let them be wrong about you     27
Burning out mind chatter (meditation reframe)     29
Happiness     31
Somebody that I used to know     33
Four years sober     35
Inner adult     37
Courage     39

| | |
|---|---:|
| Finding relief | 41 |
| A scoring system for stability | 43 |
| Lucky | 45 |
| Settled | 47 |
| Worthy | 49 |
| You know what to do | 51 |

## Part 2 Sowing The Seeds — 53

| | |
|---|---:|
| Do anything | 57 |
| Keep going | 59 |
| Everything is a choice | 61 |
| How to know what you want | 63 |
| 4:1 Game | 65 |
| Indecision | 67 |
| Obstacles or detours | 69 |
| Rubber Balls | 71 |
| Considering the opposite | 73 |
| Stillness moves mountains | 77 |
| The antidote to frustration | 81 |
| Slow your pace, unleash your joy | 83 |
| Having no opinion | 85 |
| Barely at 10 per cent | 87 |
| Simple loves | 89 |
| More | 91 |
| Lists | 93 |
| Living beyond twenty-three | 97 |
| Three alternative realities | 99 |
| Tend to your corner of the garden | 101 |

## Part 3 Allowing To Bloom — 105

| | |
|---|---|
| Swapping having for being | 109 |
| Cultivating our own wisdom | 111 |
| Magnetism | 113 |
| Broaden out in all directions | 117 |
| Guilt versus shame | 121 |
| How to make a decision (nine-step process) | 125 |
| Settling in to joy | 127 |
| Calling done at B- | 129 |
| Worry | 131 |
| Living with myself | 133 |
| Adding more 'ish to your life | 135 |
| Travelling intuitively | 137 |

## Reflections and Final Thoughts — 141

| | |
|---|---|
| Acknowledgements | 145 |
| About the author | 147 |

# Why we need courage before bravery

In a world that often tells us to be strong, to toughen up and to put on a brave face, it can be easy to confuse true courage with mere bravado. We often find ourselves caught in a constant battle between the desire to shield ourselves from vulnerability and the longing to step into the unknown, to grow and to expand. But within this dichotomy lies a crucial distinction: the difference between bravery fuelled by defensiveness and bravery fuelled by courage.

The former, fuelled by defensiveness, is an immediate reaction to the unfolding circumstances that threaten to expose our delicate sensitivities and perceived flaws. It's the kind of bravery that leads us to take fast action in a frantic attempt to avoid discomfort. In these moments, it is natural for us to default to behaviours that are controlling, manipulative and demanding, seeking quick fixes to protect ourselves.

While this kind of bravery can be necessary and helpful in certain situations—speaking up for a co-worker facing unfair treatment or risking our own safety to rescue someone in immediate physical danger—it ultimately keeps us stuck in familiar patterns. It offers a temporary shield against vulnerability but fails to foster growth and true connection.

On the other hand, bravery fuelled by courage emerges from intention and is characterised by its gentle and sustainable nature. It is an acceptance of discomfort, an acknowledgment that evolution lies in the space beyond our comfort zone. This kind of bravery allows us to pause, to sit in the liminal space between two worlds. To make deliberate choices based on what calls to our deepest selves.

**At its core, courage is the quiet and tender precursor to a kind of bravery that is generative, supportive and expansive.**

When we pause and lean in, we can find the threads of courage woven into stories of those who choose the path of growth. It is the woman who, despite her fear, walks away from a life that looks rich but feels poor. It is the artist who chooses to share their art with the world,

## INTRODUCTION

fully aware of the potential for rejection and criticism. It is the individual who speaks their truth, even when it risks challenging societal norms and facing judgment. These acts of courage may not always make headlines, but they reverberate through the lives of those who choose them, offering inspiration and transformation.

Courage is what's required to live a deep and meaningful life. It's something that's always available to us. It's simply a choice we make in the moment. To choose to be courageous doesn't mean that there's an absence of fear, it's quite the opposite. Being courageous means that we acknowledge there's risk ahead and fear is present, but we choose to take the next step towards what's calling us. With time and attention, we can cultivate the habit of choosing courage. But our familiarity with courage will take time to grow and mature. It will require a significant degree of emotional discomfort, exposure and vulnerability to develop our relationship with it and trust in it as our ally.

When we avoid the opportunities to be courageous, we stay within the seduction of safety. We refuse and reject the new beginnings that are waiting to unfold. We turn our backs on our desires and fix our gazes firmly on the past.

Courage is what moves our lives forward. It's what opens our hearts to possibility, potential and love. To be courageous, we don't have to set our lives ablaze today and burn urgently to the ground all that's been. We simply have to allow that flicker of delight to catch, to spark, to ignite. We have to allow our courage to be kindled.

This book is a threshold, but not in the sense that it separates your life in an absolute way. Rather, this threshold is the delicate and tender space between what's been, and what's in the process of becoming. I invite you to journey through this threshold with me. Together, we'll explore where we find ourselves today, what we'll leave behind and what we'll move towards.

INTRODUCTION

# Introduction

I didn't realise at the time that I was writing this book; I'd been feeling stuck creatively in my work for a while. As a coach and mentor, there was an established rhythm and routine with my clients, but there was also a lack of newness and excitement for me personally. On my usual morning walk with my dog in the trees behind our house, the beginnings of an idea sparked. I was able to catch this momentary flash of inspiration as I'd left my phone at home. With no music, no podcasts, no distractions, there was space for me to hear my own thoughts and follow their threads.

What I heard was, Do something small and often and watch it grow. Before I got home, the decision had been made. I would embark upon a 100 Day Journey, which involved daily sharing of ideas, simple practices and snippets of wisdom on the art of living well. This journey would take the form of a daily written email and an audio note that I'd send to my subscribers each morning at 9am. Staying accountable and consistent for a hundred days felt like a huge undertaking, but I remembered the instruction 'small and often'. I asked myself, What would this look like if it were easy? I reminded myself that I didn't have to write an essay each day, just a small note—something I felt inspired to share each day would be enough. Before I could overthink it, I wrote the first note that day and scheduled it to be sent at 9am the following morning.

At first, I got a few replies telling me how helpful the note was, how it was just what they needed to hear that day, how it offered comfort and possibility in seemingly hopeless situations. Then a few more replies came, and then a few more. I could feel the momentum gathering and the ripples of contribution becoming stronger. Other areas of my life began to sprout also, especially in my work. But I started to feel the familiar creep of overwhelm and obligation. I started this journey because I wanted to ignite my creativity and create opportunities for newness and adventure; this had already happened. So, I decided that my 100 Day Journey would pull into the harbour for a longer-than-planned stay at Day 50.

My notes moving forwards would be more 'postcards from my travels' rather than daily updates.

# INTRODUCTION

My 'destination' of renewed enthusiasm had already been reached, so I allowed myself to stay a while in this new place. It was a beautiful reminder to me that the purpose of a specific goal or aim isn't necessarily to get us to the destination we set before we left home. Sometimes, the inspiration to act is to simply lift us up and out from our inertia, and make us available to the myriad possibilities that await. It takes courage to start, and it takes courage to stop. Dropping anchor at Day 50 felt complete and true. I moved on with other creative projects that felt exciting and expansive.

While I was on my journey of daily notes, I was also working with a writing coach. I'd always wanted to write a book and this felt like the right time. But three different proposals, outlines and chapter summaries later, I called it quits. Maybe this wasn't the right time, after all. Then, I had another spark of inspiration. What if I'd just written a book throughout my 50 Day Journey? I selected a few example notes, made some small edits and sent the manuscript to my publisher. I shared the story of my journey of daily notes, how they'd been really well received and how I'd love to share them with a larger audience. The rest, as they say, is history. Seeds of Courage was born from these original fifty notes. There have been some edits and tweaks, as well as the addition of some new notes. I'm so honoured and grateful I get to share them with you.

# How to use this book

The rhythms and cycles of life are all around us, but often we're too busy and distracted to notice them. They're subtle, gradual and continually transforming in plain sight. But this slowness is easy to miss if we aren't paying attention. We notice suddenly the autumn trees are now all but bare of their once abundant leaves, or the tightly bound buds of flowers are now giving way to the inevitable blooming of spring.

Slowing down and being present gives us access to these small and fragile evolutions. For this reason, I've written this book in three parts to follow this natural cycling through life.

Part 1 is about tilling the soil of our life. We must tend to the ground we plan to grow our lives from. We must spend some time making space for that which we want to plant. It's in this caretaking of our own personal soil that we create the most optimal and hopeful environments to allow us to thrive.

Part 2 is where we begin to sow the seeds of what we want to grow. We must hone our vision and curate what we want to take root in this garden we've prepared lovingly.

Part 3 is where we allow our efforts to bloom. This is where the seemingly invisible becomes visible, where the energetic becomes the material, where our intentions become our reality.

From here, we return to tending to the soil again to prepare for another cycle to begin. But this is not a death; this is a deepening of what unfolded in the first cycle. We've nourished ourselves with the fruit of the first harvest and now we get to regenerate the soil and plant the seeds of new desires that have developed along the way.

For me, this idea of cyclical living has, in the past, felt repetitive and directionless. There have been many times in my life where I've believed that I've been spinning in circles, stuck in habit and sameness. But now, I see that it was simply the vantage point I was choosing to observe my life from that created this illusion. Taking a bird's-eye view of my life, it appeared that I was, in fact, going around in circles. But, when I shifted my position and came out from under the heaviness of my life, I was

# INTRODUCTION

able to view these circles for what they actually were: not simply repetitive cycles in the same place, but a beautiful upwards spiral taking me out of the old and up towards newness.

With each new spiral, we're evolving and growing. This is similar to how a tree grows stronger, taller and more deeply rooted each year, even though it goes through a phase of shedding its leaves and beginning anew.

No longer will we adorn our lives with the aesthetic glamour of cut flowers. Although they may look pleasing, there are no roots and there is no growth. They may appear beautiful, but they are essentially dead.

Creating our lives in accordance with the phases of tilling, sowing and allowing means that we will bloom from deep roots woven into fertile ground. We will have substance and a place to call home.

I suggest that you read this book from start to finish for the first time. Then, feel free to pick it up and read individual notes as you are inspired to. Having an awareness of what phase you are currently in will help you to gently release any tension you're holding and find comfort and kinship within the notes of that particular phase.

Throughout the book you will notice there are 'Ask yourself' prompts within some of the notes. These can be used as openers for your journalling practice or simply as 'thought seeds' for you to spend some time pondering as you move through your day. When it comes to these prompts, I always recommend going narrow and deep as opposed to wide and shallow. They don't have to be rushed through; there is no completion of them, as such. Give yourself space and time to study them and notice what comes up for you.

Lastly, before we begin, I encourage you to embark on this journey with a quality of mindfulness that recognises what's unfolding, then the journey becomes the very thing we hope to find at the destination.

# Part 1
# Tilling The Soil

*To prepare… to edit… to weed out… to make space… to tend to… to remove… to eliminate… to root out… to do away with… to simplify… to allow for expansion…*

The first section of this book is about clearing, editing and simplifying. The notes contained within Part 1 are written with the intention of helping us clear some space—mentally, emotionally and, at times, physically—before we start to add more to our lives.

This is a crucial step if we want to create with intention and from our internal source of knowing and nourishment, rather than being at the mercy of, and reacting to, what's happening externally. It's time to gently reorient ourselves, to set down all heavy doing and grasping action, to slow our minds and bodies and hearts, and to gradually begin experiencing the world from the inside out, not the outside in.

The importance of preparing the ground before planting new seeds and watching them grow is something that I've often learned the hard way. From deep within the uncomfortable but oh-so-familiar chaos of adding more to an already overwhelming life, I learned to retreat back to myself and tend to my life by removing what no longer belongs there and to unburden myself of any outdated responsibilities and obligations. I know now, in retrospect, this was not an error but simply a part of my learning on how to live in alignment with the natural cycle of life. Our habits can create deep grooves that require our kind attention and gentle patience for them to begin to fill in. One of the most significant examples of this learning for me was when I made the decision to remove alcohol from my life.

I decided it was time on a very ordinary Sunday in July 2018. Not time for yet another alcohol-free month which I'd done before, but time for a longer break from drinking. The months that followed were strange and uncomfortable as I navigated this new way of being me in the world, especially in social situations. I didn't know who I was without alcohol and here I was, awkwardly doing it publicly for all to see. Then something beautiful happened. My life slowed down to a delicious pace and, at the same time, it picked up momentum. I had more space, more time, more clarity and more creativity in all areas of my life. Work projects that had been on the back burner for years started to get more of my attention. I let go lovingly of some relationships that I could see had been built on the basis of alcohol, and instead nurtured new ones that were so much richer, deeper and honest.

I realised that I'd used alcohol as a way to numb myself, as a way to cope and get through life. But I didn't want to get through life, I wanted to be in my life. I wanted to be awake and present and available to the people and experiences that were all around me. I couldn't do that through the murky filter of daily drinking. I didn't have to be an alcoholic to stop drinking. I didn't have to hit some monumental rock bottom of losing my job, house, driver's licence or kids in order to make a different choice. My life with alcohol had been good by many standards. But it is so much sweeter without it.

Discomfort in life is inevitable. For me, it was the choice of being discomforted by staying where I was and continuing to exist only on the surface of my life, or the discomfort of diving deeper into who I really was at my core. Stagnation or expansion. I chose to courageously and gently move in the direction of expansion.

When we feel stuck and alone, we usually skip this vital first phase and jump straight to action. We so desperately want to feel something good, something new, to sense that spark of optimism in our belly. But before we add to our life, we need to uproot what no longer belongs there. We must clear space for the newness that's waiting to emerge. We must tend to our hearts and minds and schedules, and take time to lovingly weed out all that's been hindering our inevitable growth and blossoming.

Alcohol was like a relentless vine, snaking itself around my life, silently strangling and choking me little by little, bit by bit. This is true of almost all things we overdo—alcohol, work, food, sex, shopping. We add them to our lives in the hope that we will feel less of the emotions we'd rather avoid, such as loneliness, fear, shame and guilt. But, almost always, there's merely a fleeting whisper of joy from these indulgences, only to push us deeper into the very darkness we're trying to escape.

My relationship with alcohol was the increasingly constricting vine wrapped around my life. The courageous act of subtracting this allowed me the room to feel, to plant new seeds with intention and to begin the journey of growing into a life that was more calm, fun and exciting than I ever could've imagined.

This wide, open space is available to you, too. It will require you to look at aspects of your life through a lens of curiosity and wonder. This is an invitation to lessen the load, to free yourself from the prison of sameness. It will ask you to start to kindle your courage. Let's begin.

PART 1 - TILLING THE SOIL

# Start

First, you must allow yourself to start. We can spend days, weeks, even years in planning mode. Planning feels purposeful, diligent, considered and, most of all, safe. We can do our research, devise our plan, identify the potential bumps and design alternative routes. But there comes a time when we have to start. We have to make the call, send the email, make the announcement or ask the question.

Our natural human resistance to change means that we'll stay in what I call the 'invisible work'. This is the work we diligently tend to that's out of sight from the rest of the world. But here, in the invisible work, nothing changes, nothing grows. Any opportunity for evolution is smothered by our inertia. There's no momentum, no flow and no contribution.

Consider this a nudge to simply start—to take a step towards what you want, venturing out of the invisible and into the visible. Feel the tugging uncertainty of exposure and move, feel the bubble of potential failure and move, feel the clinging to what's known and move.

Move, just one small step, in the direction of what you want, of what feels inspired, of what feels like expansion. Emergence is a natural part of life. So today, allow yourself to emerge. Allow yourself to be courageous. Allow yourself to start.

PART 1 - TILLING THE SOIL

# Safety enables risk

In a world fuelled by urgency, fast action and the cultural idea that we should be hacking, optimising and monetising everything we do, it's all too easy to lose our centre. We can get caught up in the slipstream of the unrelenting never-enoughness we're conditioned to believe is just an inevitable part of our lives. I, too, have found myself (and still do at times) in this grasping energy of more.

> If I just had more \_\_\_\_\_,
> my life would be more \_\_\_\_\_.

More money = more success.
More clients = more influence.
More time = more joy.
More motivation = more output.

But endless action without clarity only creates more chaos and unrest. What we need is to cultivate rhythm, routine and ritual into our days. It's from the solid ground of these practices that we're then available to take the next step. When we can feel a sense of surety and certainty in our lives—by focusing our time and attention on the elements that are within our control—we give ourselves permission to take more risks, try new things, lessen the weight and consequence of our potential failures down the track. The popular 'leap, and the net will appear' approach—a phrase coined by American essayist, John Burroughs—can have a tendency to lead us to more anxiety and more fear. It has us feeling like a rubber band, stretching to its limit only to snap back to its starting position with exhaustion and increasing frailty when all doesn't go as planned.

There's a different approach. We can create a safe and fertile garden from which to bloom. We don't make good decisions from fear, anger, blame or doubt. We need to move our way gradually, courageously, from fear to hope. And then, from a home of optimism, wonder and excitement, we can afford ourselves the gift of risk with a clear mind, clear thoughts, clear intention. We don't have to know how to achieve what we most want right now, in this very moment. We just need the clarity of intention and a process to move towards that desire—hour by hour, day by day. This is the gift of routine.

**Ask yourself:**
- Where can I build routine into my days?
- What beats can I teach my body and mind to expect as a way of signalling that all is well and that I actually do have control—even in unpredictable times?

PART 1 - TILLING THE SOIL

# Joyful discomfort

Discomfort is an inevitable part of life. I know, I'm not selling the dream here! Living in discomfort doesn't sound all that fun or particularly exciting. It can feel like the opposite direction to the way that we want to be travelling, but stay with me…

Embracing discomfort makes our lives flow more freely. I often like to think of it as the discomfort we experience when we start a new exercise program, or we start running for the first time, or we start lifting weights at the gym. We know and expect there to be physical discomfort from this new exercise. There's an expectation of discomfort and we often welcome it. We want it to be there because we can recognise it as an indication that we're making progress, that something is changing, that we're developing. We're literally getting physically stronger and fitter.

When we look at discomfort, we have two options:

**Option A:** we can choose the discomfort of change.

**Option B:** we can choose the discomfort of staying where we are.

We're going to experience discomfort either way. But we get to choose which flavour of discomfort we opt for. It's easy for us to view the physical discomfort of exercise in this way, but what if we could apply the same principle to emotional discomfort? Again, we can experience Option A: the emotional discomfort of change, showing up in different ways, practising having different thoughts and holding different beliefs about things, questioning our choices and if they're aligned with where we want to move into. Or, we can choose Option B: the emotional discomfort of staying where we are, not making any changes, remaining locked in habitual thoughts and beliefs that will simply keep repeating themselves and affecting our lives.

If we want to lead deep, connected, meaningful lives, we must acknowledge that discomfort is inevitable. As humans, we're going to experience discomfort; there's no escaping it. But we get to choose which type of discomfort we're going to experience. The discomfort of change has potential sewn into it, while the discomfort of stagnation, of sameness, has us feeling hopeless.

**Ask yourself:**
- How would I navigate today if I embraced the inevitability of discomfort?
- What would I do?
- Where would I go?
- What would I say?
- To whom would I say those things?

PART 1 - TILLING THE SOIL

## You are the narrator

What story are you telling about your life? This is a question I've asked myself repeatedly over the past decade. Sometimes I've liked the answer, and other times I haven't. It can be confronting to see yourself from the outside looking in. We can find ourselves living in ways that are off track, misaligned and out of sync with who we really want to be in the world. There are two ways to approach this question. We can look at it with past focus—where we take stock of all the decisions we've made, failures we've encountered, heartbreaks we've endured, unfairness we've experienced—and we can use these stories to determine who we are today, in this moment. Or, we can look at it with future focus—to focus on who we are becoming—using the contrast we've experienced in the past simply as a tool to better refine the kind of life we want to create.

In my own life, I could look back and paint a pretty bleak picture of my life up to this point. I could tell the story of being a divorced mother of two. I could tell the story of being a woman who has experienced the extreme ebbs and flows of business over the past decade, who at times had to decide if she used what was available in the bank to either pay the water bill or to buy a birthday gift for her son, not both. I could tell the story of being isolated from extended family and having to navigate motherhood without the help of older women who'd travelled this path before me. I could tell the story of being an alcoholic who had to get sober or risk losing everything.

I'm sure you can feel the helplessness of these stories. I know I can. The truth is, at times, I've identified with these powerless versions of my story. I've used them as fuel for my self-pitying narrative, to justify and give reason for feeling stuck and disempowered. But now, I choose to tell a different story of my past that in turn creates a much more optimistic and peaceful present and lays the path for a much more joyful and abundant future. With this future focus, I'm able to tell a different story.

I'm a mother of two who has created a family structure that allows everyone to thrive. I'm a woman who has cultivated a relationship with her ex-husband that enables respectful, honest co-parenting of two amazing humans. I'm a woman who has made hard decisions that have allowed her to become more of who she truly is—even when the outcome has been uncertain. I'm a woman who has left relationships that are good by many standards, but where she had to be less than who she was to fit into the space that was given to her. I'm a woman who has learned to have her own back, even when nobody else did. I'm a woman who doesn't need the lubricant of alcohol to feel joy and connection.

PART 1 - TILLING THE SOIL

With forward focus, we can reframe our past. It's not set in stone. We get to change the story about who we were then, who we are today and who we're becoming. We're all the narrators of our own stories.

**Ask yourself:**
- What weak, disempowered and hopeless stories about my life am I ready to allow to dissolve?
- What bold, powerful and dynamic stories about my life do I want to shine a light on?

PART 1 - TILLING THE SOIL

# Let them be wrong about you

I used to be the most easily offended person. I'd take everything personally. If someone offered criticism or even what I perceived to be negative feedback about my work or writing or podcast, I'd either believe what that person said and feel deep shame and guilt, or I'd go into full defensive and justification mode, making them wrong so I could be right. Not anymore.

I've decided to let people be wrong about me. I no longer try to convince them otherwise. And let me tell you, it's deliciously liberating. Someone else's opinion doesn't automatically make it true for me.

A few months ago, I was having a particularly difficult conversation with someone.

They said, 'I don't mean to offend you, but… [insert potentially offensive statement here!]' Sidenote: this preface is up there with 'I'm not gossiping, but…' What happened next was both surprising and delightful.

In that split second, a little voice inside me said, This is interesting. I wonder what they're going to say… I knew that whatever they said didn't have the power to offend me because I didn't have to believe it. I didn't have to agree with them or make them wrong. It was a moment of pure freedom. Freedom from having to be understood by everyone. Freedom from feeling the need to justify myself. Freedom from allowing anything external to dictate my inner state.

I encourage you to let people be wrong about you. Let them have their opinion. Let them blame you, if they must. Then, decide that it means nothing about you. Decide to be unoffendable. This is a superpower that is available to us all, but few embrace. Allow them to be who they are. Then, smile and get on with being who you are. No resentment, no judgement, just love.

PART 1 - TILLING THE SOIL

# Burning out mind chatter (meditation reframe)

It can be easy to beat ourselves up for not being 'better' at meditation. We know it should be about clearing the mind and getting into the space of non-thinking. But have you tried that when you've got seventy-three things to get done that day, you already feel like you're behind schedule and it's not even 9am?

Sure, with a full sixty minutes ahead of you, no-one demanding your attention (bosses, kiddos, the dentist's text reminder about that appointment at 1pm today…) and nowhere to be, we *might* be able to sit long enough to reach blissful stillness and non-doing, but we don't always have the capacity for that. And the good news is, you don't have to in order to reap the rewards of a meditation practice.

My daily practice is between ten and twenty minutes each morning, and another ten minutes later in the afternoon. There were times in the past where I'd get mad with myself for still feeling fidgety when the timer went off. If I tried to sit for longer, it only resulted in me feeling more frazzled, not less. It was time for a reframe.

What if… sitting for fifteen minutes, simply being aware of the franticness of my thoughts, helped me to *burn them out?* What if… this container allowed me to *use up* the noisy chatter so it didn't impact the rest of my day? What if… I viewed these ten minutes as a sort of ritualistic campfire—for me to toss all the unhelpful, fear-based thoughts and familiar old patterns of stuckness and not-enoughness into the flames and *dissolve them?*

Meditation has allowed me to recommit day after day to my gentle practice with a sense of non-attachment. Everything that comes up in your meditation practice is helpful. Everything that comes up is useful. Everything that comes up is in service of you. Meditation is a practice to clear the clutter and allow more clarity.

I invite you to sit at your own campfire, allow the chatter to be there and know that you're offering these thoughts to be burned out so you can have access to more spaciousness and lightness of mind as you move through your day.

PART 1 - TILLING THE SOIL

# Happiness

If you could be happy every day for the rest of your life, would you choose that? It seems like a fairly odd question, right? Given the opportunity, who wouldn't want to feel consistently happy?

The truth is, there are many circumstances that we will find ourselves in where we wouldn't choose happiness, even if it were available.

**For example:**
- On hearing a terminal medical diagnosis of a loved one.
- On discovering the job that we so dearly wanted went to someone else.
- On receiving a call from school to say there was an accident and you're needed, now.
- On witnessing a crash on the freeway where three family cars were involved.
- On hearing that there's nothing else they can do and you should start to make plans.

In these scenarios, it's an act of great kindness to allow ourselves to experience all of the emotions that come up: sadness, confusion, terror, helplessness. I believe that what we're really seeking is peace—to welcome peace in the face of despair, frustration, discontent, stagnation,

*31*

grief, shame. What we crave is a broader, more textured human experience.

We want to know that we can feel these intense emotions and that we'll still be okay. We'll survive. We can hold them, witness them and allow them to be present.

The extent to which we can allow deep grief is the same extent to which we can feel joy and bliss. Allowing the grief and sadness to be there gives us the opportunity for it to be transmuted and to pass. The more we resist and push against it, the more ferocity it gathers and the more persistent it becomes.

Rather than striving for happiness, what if we allowed our hearts to settle on the emotion that was asking to be felt, and held space for that emotion with an offering of peace?

Grief and peace.

Sadness and peace.

Confusion and peace.

Loneliness and peace.

Frustration and peace.

PART 1 - TILLING THE SOIL

# Somebody that I used to know

I used to be someone who…

- Booked a last-minute flight to some far-off corner of the world.
- Found it really easy to make a decision.
- Was spontaneous and adventurous.
- Was curious and fascinated by people and the world.
- Laughed easily.
- Cried easily.
- Knew what they wanted.
- Was willing to fail.

Now, it's your turn to fill in the blank.

I used to be someone who_____.

What I know to be true from my own experience is the more responsibility we take on, the less tolerance or capacity we have for risk. When there's more at stake, we take less chances. This is what so many of us experience in our 30s—with perhaps the house and the marriage and the kids and the career and the routine—in a life that feels increasingly heavy and laden with burden and obligation.

The natural resistance to change that humans have means it's easy to look around and confirm that we're right and virtuous for being 'responsible', for not risking what we've created. But where are you settling for less than what you truly want? Where are you using responsibility as an excuse to turn your back on yourself and the life you truly want to create? What if your greatest expression of responsibility was a commitment to growth and expansion? What if you deemed it the most responsible act to be an example of someone who is responsible and who has cultivated a willingness to embrace uncertainty? What if you allowed your capacity for risk to grow at the same pace as your growing responsibilities?

**Ask yourself:**
- What would that version of me say 'yes' to?
- What would that version of me be willing to try?
- What would that version of me turn their face towards and move closer to?

PART 1 - TILLING THE SOIL

# Four years sober

I want you to know that you don't have to wait until you hit rock bottom to make a different choice.

Last week* marked four years since I decided to remove alcohol from my life. Aside from all the expected benefits—better sleep, health, mood, skin—one of the most beautiful gifts over the past four years has been that I've learned to trust myself more than I ever have before. I have my own back. I do what I say I'm going to do. I feel confident in being able to show up for myself when I need myself the most.

Quitting drinking has allowed me to parent myself, to look after myself, to be there for myself in a way that's loving, gentle and kind. And I can show up for my sons with that same tenderness and awareness. It's the boldest act of radical kindness I've gifted my family.

Unhealthy, dependent relationships with alcohol are present on both sides of my family. The visibly destructive addictions were obviously problematic, but other times the dependency was more obscure, subtler, harder to detect, as the person presented to the world as highly functioning and successful.

It made it difficult as a child to identify alcohol as a potential problem, as there were so many different environments where it was being used—to numb, to distract, to connect, to celebrate.

What I've learned over the years is that time slows to the drip of honey without alcohol, and in the most delicious way. There's less urgency, rush and chaos and more time to savour, ponder and consider. In times of intensity, there's more space to pause and decide my next step. And in the more simple and ordinary moments, there's more space to savour the beauty and magic of life, especially with the people I love.

Alcohol was a handbrake on my life. Releasing that handbrake has allowed all that's good to flow to me, and all that needs to be released to dissolve.

It's brought me into greater alignment with myself—which alcohol had me abandon continuously—and, bit by bit, allowed me to feel worthy and available to this most magical and gentle life I get to experience.

*Original note published 12 July, 2022*

PART 1 - TILLING THE SOIL

# Inner adult

I'm seeing and hearing a lot about our inner child at the moment. Specifically, the need to heal our inner child and process the trauma and grief that this child version of us has experienced. This concept has never sat all that well with me.

Yes, I acknowledge the power of reflection and unpacking the beliefs that we developed in our childhood. But this information needs to be used in the present moment to move us forwards.

The common narrative seems to stop at the reflection and unpacking stage. There's little practical advice around what we should then *do*, the actions we should take from that place of awareness and understanding.

I recently* attended a lecture with author Marianne Williamson. She spoke to this idea of healing our inner child. She was able to articulate perfectly what I've felt around this topic. She said, 'It's sad when a child doesn't experience childhood. But it's pathetic when an adult doesn't experience adulthood.' She was direct, clear, honest.

If our gaze is fixed only on what happened (or didn't happen) back then—if we get stuck ruminating on what *should* have been better, how it *should* have been—we miss the beauty and opportunity available to us here, in the present moment, and also for what lies ahead.

I believe that we all have some form of trauma from our childhood. But we have a choice whether or not we let that trauma rob us of the life we want to create as adults. It's not about denying what happened in our childhood or burying our head in the sand. But there has to be both the reflection and processing *and* then the future visioning and gentle steps towards who we want to become and what we want to be an example of in the world.

Rumination can feel comfortable in its familiarity. It can give us a sense of safety and security. But it can be the invisible weight that we carry though our days, which makes it impossible to feel free. It's about gently shifting our awareness from looking to our past and inner child and tenderly reorienting ourselves towards our future and inner adult.

Who might you be if you spend time becoming familiar with your inner adult, rather than tending endlessly to your inner child?

*\* Original note published 9 August, 2022*

PART 1 - TILLING THE SOIL

# Courage

We all admire people that we deem to be courageous and brave. But yet, when faced with the opportunity to practise courage and bravery ourselves, we all too often shy away. We plough ahead, business as usual. We distract ourselves—often with busyness and any form of 'overing'. Over-working, over-drinking, over-eating, over-exercising, over-talking, over-analysing, over-teching.

The very fact that we require courage in a situation means that we're moving into unchartered waters. And, in this new space, we will most likely feel fearful—fearful of an undesired result or response. We hold ourselves back from doing the courageous thing because if we do, then what? If we can't control the outcome or the reaction, then what?

Courage is a choice. Courage says, *I can't be certain of the outcome but I'm willing to go there*. Courage says, *This is outside of my comfort zone but I'm going to take the next step*. Courage says, *This is what's true for me and I don't know how you'll respond, but I'm going to have my own back*.

We embody courage when we say the unsaid thing. We've all experienced conversations where we know we're skirting around what *actually* has to be said. Courage is taking a step towards yourself and standing in the uncomfortable open space. Courage is speaking one small sentence of truth and then staying in the discomfort of the silence. Courage is saying 'no' with grace and honesty when you've always said 'yes', and then not apologising or justifying your response.

    I invite you to practise courage today with one small act. Take one small step outside of what's familiar. Speak one simple truth aloud. Then, notice the expanse of the moment that follows being courageous.

PART 1 - TILLING THE SOIL

# Finding relief

I used to (until fairly recently) shun the idea of a quick fix in order to feel better. I firmly believed that life hacks never worked and only offered temporary solutions at best. But, what if some temporary relief is just what you need to move up the emotional scale a few notches? What if this is exactly what you need so you can settle on solid ground and look at the bigger picture? What if this gives you sure footing to make calmer, more deliberate choices for the longer term?

When you know how to shift your energy just a few degrees from frustration to contentment, from contentment to hopefulness, you start moving in the right direction. Because we all make clearer choices from a place of hopefulness than from one of frustration. And that's actually what we want to feel: a sense of movement towards what we want.

Here are some ways that you can offer yourself relief today:

- **Get into a body of water.** It doesn't matter if it's a swimming pool, a bath, the ocean, a lake, a pond—just get into some water.
- **Raise your heart rate.** Go for a run, do a movement class, dance.

- **Listen to an uplifting podcast.**
- **Watch something funny online.** This is a sure-fire way to shift any heavy energy and lift your mood.
- **Make or order some easy, delicious food.** If making food is too hard for you today, then order something nourishing.
- **Listen to music that makes you feel alive.**
- **Write lists of things that you love.**
- **Write lists of times that you felt joyful.**
- **Write lists of amazing things that you've accomplished in your work.**
- **Play an instrument or learn something new.**
- **Draw or paint or sketch.**
- **Get up a little earlier.** Get outside before the day starts and before you get into work.
- **Make gentle plans.** Connect with just one or two supportive people over the coming days.
- **Plan a trip or a holiday that you really want to take.**

Sometimes helping ourselves feel better is the first step of progress. Leave the heavy stuff for today and instead do something to move yourself up the emotional scale. You'll feel a whole lot more stable and capable of looking at some of the heavier stuff tomorrow.

PART 1 - TILLING THE SOIL

# A scoring system for stability

Disregard the extremes at either end of the emotional scale, and then take an average of what's left. You see this kind of scoring system in gymnastics—the highest and lowest scores are thrown out and an average is taken of what remains. This is the way to get the most accurate representation of a situation. (Yes, there are other elements to the gymnastics scoring system, but I'll not pretend to know how it all works!)

This concept got me thinking about how we might apply it in our lives. We can often identify with the worst parts of our life: that job we got fired from, the breakup, the failed business… Or, we can identify with the best parts of our life: getting the promotion, being part of the winning team, signing the dream client.

We're not our accomplishments, but they do significantly impact our sense of self and the identity we have in the world. But what if we applied this scoring system to our lives? What if we disregarded these sharp highs and deep lows, and instead took an average of what's left?

How would our opinion change if, at the end of the year, we stopped focusing on the most significant high and the most painful low? Would we like what we're left with?

Recently, I've been playing with this concept on a smaller scale. At the end of each day, I've been applying this 'scoring system'. What I'm learning is that life is pretty consistent and balanced when we stop fixating on the extremes. It's calmer when we can reduce the impact these occasional, fleeting moments have—both the ecstatic joy *and* the deep disappointment.

This approach is not saying that we'll never experience these 'far ends of the scale' situations. What it does mean is that we'll give them less power over how we feel about ourselves and our place in the world. It reorients us towards the stable, solid and reliable. When we do this, we're much better equipped to deal with the lows and also avoid becoming addicted to chasing the highs. It's shown me just how beautifully plain and simple life can be.

**Ask yourself:**
- What are the recurring themes and patterns that emerge when I disregard the extremes of life?
- What does the story of my day, week, month, year look like through this lens?

PART 1 - TILLING THE SOIL

# Lucky

'You're so lucky.' This is a phrase I'd hear often when on the phone with my mum. She would ask how life was—work, the kids, the trip we'd just returned from—and the response was always the same: lucky, so lucky.

Yes, I was aware of the privileges I had. I had the freedom to live in Australia, own a home, have children and a business, but the truth is, I felt lonely, depressed and numbed out from the life that was orbiting me.

There have been many times I've felt this dissonance between what my life *looks like to others* and what it *feels like to me*. One of these times was when I was in my early 30s. My life looked like something to admire on the surface. I was living in a four-bedroom home in an idyllic little beachside pocket just outside of Melbourne, with trees, lovely neighbours, good schools and the ocean nearby. I was married to a good guy, had two healthy children and a business that was growing, I went to regular yoga classes and spent weekends watching my kids play sports, visiting markets and attending dinners and birthday parties. Yet, I'd never felt so deeply sad and alone.

It's possible for our lives to *look* full and *feel* empty. And ironically, the more heavily we pack our schedules, the more disconnected we tend to feel. Our habitual gravitation towards busyness anaesthetises our senses, numbing us to what's asking for our time, attention, care and nurturance.

Know this: you're allowed to acknowledge your privilege, and also want more. You're not bound to a life that you've outgrown. You're allowed to move through the seasons of your life, being present to the natural ebb and flow of each and then welcoming the next with wonder, curiosity and receptivity.

**Ask yourself:**
- Am I clutching onto a season that naturally wants to give way to what's waiting to unfold?

# Settled

If we're not careful, we can spend our entire lives trying exhaustedly to get to a place other than where we are. We do this because we imagine 'over there' to be better than where we are in this moment.

Life will be better when… We finish this sentence in a multitude of ways. When I'm married, when I'm divorced, when I have children, when my children grow up, when I have more time for my work , when I have more time with my family.

We're not living when we're in this constant striving for what we don't have yet; we're merely existing. In a conversation with a dear friend, she was talking about the many moving parts of her life at the moment and how she yearned for things to feel settled.

There's such beautiful relief in feeling settled. That running to-do list dissolves, we have more space, our capacity to love and be present in our interactions is amplified.

We have a tendency to want to go from one end of the scale to the other. From frantic and overwhelmed all the way to calm and serene. From hopeless and lost to vibrant and connected. But we place little value on the space between these two extremes. There's great comfort and peace to be found in the more neutral emotions on the scale: relief, ease, contentment, stability, settled.

These states of being aren't awarded to us when we get to our final destination. They're not external things to be won or given. They're ways of being that are available to us no matter where we are on our journey.

What if you called this place that you stand in right now, settled? What if you choose to cultivate the essence of being settled without requiring anything external to change?

You can have dreams, aspirations and desires that haven't come to fruition yet, and still choose to feel settled. It's always a choice and always available to us if we choose to orient ourselves towards it.

There's great comfort in knowing that we'll always have desires that haven't materialised yet. Our nature as humans is that as soon as we realise one dream, our imagination inspires us to focus on something else that's new, exciting and not quite within reach at the moment. This isn't cause to feel lack; this is an invitation to be satisfied with where we are and eager for what's to come.

**Ask yourself:**
- Where am I craving to feel settled in my life at the moment?

You might find it helpful to complete this sentence: *'Once I have/fix/get/complete/let go of/achieve_____, then I'll feel settled.'* Hone in on the external circumstance that you're attaching your peace to, and then choose to call it settled, in all its imperfect unfolding.

PART 1 - TILLING THE SOIL

# Worthy

What would you do today if you felt worthy? What would you say 'no' to? What would you say 'yes' to? What would you give less attention to? What would be granted more of your love and energy?

The feeling of unworthiness can disguise itself cunningly as confusion. We convince ourselves that we don't know what to do in the particularly tricky situation we might be facing. Yes, sometimes we need more time—we need to feel into what our next right move is—but more often than not, we know what we need to do or want to do. We keep our hearts imprisoned in an eternal waiting room, never moving forwards in the direction of what's tugging gently at our hearts.

When we indulge in this confusion, we disallow the exploration of what we truly want because, at our core, we don't feel worthy of it. Underneath our confusion—whether that's what job to take, what house to buy, what trip to go on or even what restaurant to eat at—is a frightened and shaky voice telling us to outsource our preferences, often defaulting to taking a poll of whomever is in the room and handing them the power to decide for us.

You're worthy of your choices. You're worthy to have your voice be heard. Your worthiness is not conditional on the approval of others. You're your own source of certainty and knowing. You don't need to justify your worthiness to create the life you so deeply want to create. Your worthiness of joy, peace and freedom are here, woven into the moments that go on to make up your life.

All is well. All is available. All is right and true and good. All of this is *for you*, never against you. Everything that's unfolding is here to guide you to what you want the most. You don't have to search endlessly for it. It's here for you whenever you're ready. Your job is to simply release the resistance that's holding you back from what's trying to come to the surface. It's time to loosen the grip, to allow the confusion to dissolve, to soften the control you've been conditioned to believe is helpful and necessary, and to slowly and gradually allow your inherent worth to be your guide.

You do know what you want. And you're unconditionally worthy of receiving it all.

PART 1 - TILLING THE SOIL

# You know what to do

It's okay that it's taken you some time to get to this knowing. There have been no missteps on your part. You've known it to be so, but you haven't been ready to take action on it. This isn't just okay, but necessary. Rash decisions made from frustration and anger are rarely acts of kindness towards ourselves. You've taken your time, you've course-corrected and explored potentials and you've been understanding and patient with others. But this attention to what others want and need comes at a cost when it's at odds with what your heart knows and wants.

No longer are you grieving for what could unfold, because it's already faded. What lies ahead will require your courage to take the next step and not retreat to this uncomfortable yet known place you've been in for so long. This is an opportunity to take one small step in the direction of what you want and then find your feet on this new ground. You don't need to be fearful. This is all for you. You're not leaving this familiar place for nothing. This isn't as good as it gets. Your job isn't to try to fit yourself into places that you're too big for. This is a reclamation of your agency. This is an opening for you to reorient yourself, be grateful for what you've learned and to know that there's more magic around the corner. All you have to do is to make space for this newness to arrive. You don't have to know what form it will take.

This is how you live fully! This is what it means to kindle your courage! There's such wonder, awe, love, depth, passion and connection waiting for you whenever you're ready. And you *are* ready.

You're more intrigued about what awaits than sad about what you're leaving behind. The balance has shifted. You're ready for so much more. You have so much more lined up and waiting for you. There's a love that you don't have to manage, earn or twist yourself into knots in order to receive. You don't have to apologise or justify why you want what you want.

You've taken such significant steps towards this life. It's time to untether yourself from what you thought you wanted and let yourself flow towards the life that's waiting for you, that's aligned and has an energy of its own. You don't have to generate the river, it's there for you to ease yourself into and be taken downstream. You're powerful, dynamic, playful, expressive and full with life. It's time to let this move you. Stop trying to move it. Let yourself be moved. Hand it all over. Just open your mouth and let the words be spoken for you. Stand and let yourself be walked. Lie and let yourself be slept. It's time to allow life to unfold for you.

# Part 2
# Sowing The Seeds

*To design... to plant... to create... to set the intention...
to invent... to map out... to germinate... to outline...
to bring into form... to cultivate*

Now that you've tilled the soil of your life and created space in your heart, mind, home and schedule, it's time to start considering what seeds you'd like to sow in this newly reclaimed fertile ground. But before we proceed, a suggestion: Not every rediscovered space needs to be filled immediately. I offer this snippet of advice here because oftentimes, when we have a new sense of spaciousness, it can feel entirely uncomfortable. There's a tendency to scramble to quickly wedge in new things, people and responsibilities to bring us back to common ground. But this delicate moment is a beautiful opportunity to practise being in spaces between; between the subtraction and addition, between the old and the new, between the inspiration and the realisation.

So, let yourself rest here for a moment. Let your awareness adjust to the new capacity you now have. It's in this place that you may experience the urge to rush, the temptation to fill up life again. Just know that there's time. There's time for you to take a breath, to lay down the anxiety and fear that comes from the illusion that you need to catch up with your own life and be further along than you are right now.

I felt this sense of urgency to act in my own life when my ex-husband and I decided to complete our ten-year marriage. We each found ourselves in our own individual spaces between, as we transitioned our relationship from husband and wife to co-parents of our two sons. This restructuring came with a seemingly endless list of decisions to be made and changes to action, including creating a two-home family. With the help of some friends and my soon-to-be ex-husband, I moved out of the family home we had bought together just a couple of years before and into a little rental property a few kilometres away.

I'll never forget the day I moved into that house. It was the first time I'd ever signed a lease by myself, the only place I'd lived where I was the only person with a key. This would be where my sons and I would figure out how to navigate this new way of being a family. They would spend one week with me at 'Mum's house', and then go to 'Dad's house' for the week, which, until recently, had simply been called 'home'.

## PART 2 - SOWING THE SEEDS

The tiny blue house, as it's always been known, was a far cry from the four-bedroom home I'd left behind. A typical little Australian weatherboard holiday house, it was draughty in winter and like a sauna in summer. The kitchen had just five little cabinets on the walls and a few shelves made out of old pieces of wood. The cheap laminate floor in the lounge was creaky and uneven, and the scratchy blue carpet tiles felt more like an office space than a home. There were three small bedrooms: one for me, one for the boys to share and one that would be my office. I offered the boys their own rooms—they'd never shared before and I wanted them to have as much continuity as possible between Mum's house and Dad's house—but they said 'no', they wanted to share. I got it. Separate rooms with closed doors in a new house with a new family structure was too much change. Let's be where we can see each other and hear each other.

Standing in the kitchen of that house, looking out at the view of the bay, I felt the richest I'd ever been. I was creating this life. I'd courageously uprooted what was known, familiar, safe and essentially 'good' by many standards, and now I was beginning to plant new seeds. I was intentionally cultivating a life that felt truer, bolder and more in line with who I was beginning to allow myself to become.

It would've been easy to look at the tiny blue house as a backwards step—a fall from grace, something to be embarrassed about or feel shame over. The cliché tale of the single mum who was forced to downsize. But I was so blissfully content and at peace in that house. I loved it. I had downsized the house but upgraded the home inside of me. The spark of knowing in my heart had caught fire and it was starting to burn.

A meaningful life isn't defined by what it *looks* like, but rather what it *feels* like.

With that, my friend, I bid you bon voyage. May your journey through this phase of sowing your own seeds of intention bring you all the joy, peace and freedom of the tiny blue house. Let's begin.

PART 2 - SOWING THE SEEDS

# Do anything

There have been times in my life where I've felt incredibly lost. That feeling of not knowing, of wanting to take action but having no idea what you'd like to do, comes with a whole lot of hopelessness and fear. Fear of time running out. Fear of never finding that spark of joy again. Fear of being unnecessary and ineffective. So, what do we do in these times? My suggestion is anything. Do anything.

This isn't the time to lean into isolation. This is the time to get out in the world and be around people. This isn't the time to prioritise solitude. This is the time to put ourselves out there in the way of opportunity.

I'm not suggesting self-abandonment, where you avoid being with yourself and your feelings. I highly recommend you bookend your day with time *with* yourself. This could be a simple fifteen-minute morning meditation practice, and some journalling time in the evening. But in the in-between, get out and be in the world.

Ask people questions, put up your hand to volunteer, help a friend. You may feel tender and vulnerable and perhaps a little fragile, and that's okay. Nothing has gone wrong. Find ways to contribute, to be of service, to be useful.

Anything… Do anything.

When we choose to lock ourselves away from the world during these seasons of uncertainty, we can't help but stay fixated on the problem—on what's wrong, on what's missing. So distract yourself from the problem for a little while. Not in a destructive way, but rather a loving way. There's time. There's more. There's space.

Anything… Do anything.

Then, watch as the Universe rearranges things to offer you glimmers of inspiration and a gentle nudge towards what's next for you.

Anything… Do anything.

PART 2 - SOWING THE SEEDS

# Keep going

Some of us are really good at starting. We take the first step into a new, unknown space. But then, we retreat back to safety—to the known and familiar.

Similar to a rubber band, we stretch out into the new space and then spring back to where we are more comfortable. I know this has been true for me in my life. I've followed that inspiration and taken the first step, but then, the vastness of the new, unchartered waters feels overwhelming, so I retreat back to the perceived safety of the familiar.

This may show up for you in work or creative projects, where you create something, tell a few people about it and then never mention it again. It may be in relationships, where you open the door to a courageous conversation about what's on your mind and in your heart, and then close the door with silence. It might show up for you in your exercise and movement routine, where you sign up for the program, buy the new gear, carve out time in your schedule and then turn your attention away from it and towards something else.

Progress is made through the courage of continuing to show up and take the next step, day after day. It's about finding home in a new place, cultivating a sense of safety there and then taking the next step, again and again and again.

There's no finish line, no final destination. It's about moving our lives forward with intention, kindness and nurturance, little by little, bit by bit. Until one day, we awake in a brand new reality—without the chaos, but instead with calm and wonderment.

PART 2 - SOWING THE SEEDS

# Everything is a choice

The to-do list, the endless checklist, the densely packed calendar—I want you to consider that everything listed is entirely optional. I want you to start to reframe things that you tell yourself you *have* to do into things that you *get* to do. This one small shift can take you immediately out of obligation and into appreciation. Rather than looking at our circumstances as things that we have to do, we get to look at them as things that we get to do. We get to feel empowered by them.

Some examples:
- We don't have to make our kids packed lunches for school. We get to make our kids packed lunches for school. We get to fill their lunch boxes with fresh food to help them grow.
- We don't have to walk our dog each day. We get to go outside into nature, breathe in the fresh air, move our body and be outside with our pet.
- We don't have to go to the gym. We get to go to the gym. We get to appreciate, love and use these healthy, strong bodies that we have and make them as resilient as possible as we move through this life.

If you have small kids at home, perhaps you're having to de-prioritise work at the moment. This is true for many of my clients. But rather than feeling this sense of *I **have*** *to look after my babies while they're small*, you could reframe it into *I **get*** *to de-prioritise my work while my babies are small*. This creates an entirely different energy. It takes us out of that victim mentality and puts us firmly in the driver's seat of our own life.

So, play with that today.

**Ask yourself:**
- Where can I reframe all of the things that I feel that I have to do into things that I get to do?

This really does transform obligation into appreciation.

PART 2 - SOWING THE SEEDS

# How to know what you want

What do you want? This question sounds simple enough. But it's not always easy to articulate. In a sea of endless possibilities, it can be overwhelming to settle on a few options when it comes to identifying what we want.

Asking this question has had a huge impact on my life. In times when I feel disconnected from the big picture, when I feel pulled down in the granular, insignificant details of the day-to-day, when I feel lost as to where I should be headed, this practice grounds me and settles me back into the knowing of my heart.

I invite you to take a piece of paper and draw a line down the middle.

On the left, write a list of all the things you *don't* want. This can be around a specific area of your life—work, relationships, health, finances—or from a broader perspective of your life.

Be specific.

What exactly is it about your current reality that you don't want?

Then, on the other side of the page, I invite you to write the opposite—everything that you *do* want.

**Let me give you some examples:**

- *I don't want to have to scramble to pay my bills every month*

becomes

- *I want to be able to pay my bills with ease every month.*

- *I don't want a partner who's so uncertain and indecisive.*

becomes

- *I want a partner who's certain and makes decisions easily and quickly.*

- *I don't want to have to spend so much time chasing invoices from my clients.*

becomes

- *I want to bring someone on to my team to manage the invoicing for my business.*

- *I don't want to have to initiate all the important conversions in my relationship.*

becomes

- *I want a partner who's willing to initiate courageous conversations with me.*

Contrast is helpful. It's a doorway to clarity and refinement of the details of our lives. When we know what we don't want, we know more of what we do want.

PART 2 - SOWING THE SEEDS

## 4:1 Game

So much of what we yearn for is outside of us. It's 'over there'. It's that big ship that appears oh-so-tiny, way off on that distant horizon. Yes, we should absolutely have goals, dreams, things, people and places to aspire to and move towards. But this mentality can drift into murky waters when we want something because we believe that we'll be happier, more joyful and more complete when we have it.

It might be a better job or more clients. It might be a partner… and then a fiancé… and then a husband or a wife… and then a divorce.

The energy of desire sends us a message that there's something we want that we don't have yet. I'm not suggesting that we stop desiring, that we stop having dreams. But we need to blend this healthy, striving energy with an energy of appreciation and gratitude for what we already have.

It's easy to forget that all of the things we have in this moment were once dreams, desires and hopes that were 'out there' in the future. So much of what we have now—whether it's the partner, the house, the health, the car, the business or the career—were once things that were simply a desire, a wish inside our heart.

I invite you to play in this little practice that I call the 4:1 Game. Take a piece of paper and write the numbers 1 to 20, one line for each number down the page. Next to the numbers 5, 10, 15 and 20, write something that you want: a desire, a goal, a wish, something that you want to create in your life. Now, next to all the other numbers, fill in these lines with things that you once wanted and you now have.

This is a magical practice. It allows us to blend the manifested with the yet-to-manifest. It dilutes that grasping, yearning energy of reaching for more. We can have a hundred things going well in our life and only one or two things that are going not-so well. And it's those one or two things that get the majority of our attention. We give more energy to what's wrong or what's missing than to what's right and what's present. This practice really imbues our desires with a strong energy of gratitude for all of the elements that we already have to appreciate.

We shouldn't stop wanting, we shouldn't stop striving. We can't—it's part of what makes us human. The very energy that will help us realise these goals, dreams and desires is in the gratitude and appreciation of the magic we've already created.

PART 2 - SOWING THE SEEDS

# Indecision

Indecision… it can feel like the most uncomfortable place to be stuck. You know that feeling of when you're weighing up all your options, you're writing your pros and cons lists, you're asking the people close to you, 'What do you think I should do?'

Those people will try to be helpful because they love you and want you to make the best decision. So they'll often tell you what they *think* you want to hear. Or, some people might tell you what *they* would do in the same situation, which, of course, might be completely different to your unique situation.

So we poll, we survey, we ponder and we deliberate. And then we stop. I see this all the time with clients. They'll do all the hard work and then stop. They freeze at the point where they need to make a choice. We all know people who live their entire lives like this—talking about all the things they want to do and then never taking that first step towards them. Here's the way I like to approach this—with my clients and with myself when I can't decide, because I too find myself here at times.

Firstly, give yourself some grace. Making decisions is a skill we have to practise. It's like a muscle we have to train. Make a decision to *not* make a decision for a set period of time. We're already feeling overwhelmed and confused, so we don't need to add more pressure to this. What we need to do is find some relief and some space.

It's from this space that we'll be able to make more informed decisions with confidence and surety. You might decide that you'll not make a decision on a particular topic for the next forty-eight hours. That's it… for the next forty-eight hours, it's off the table.

Making a decision to *not* make a decision *is* making a decision! The relief and spaciousness this opens up lets us find our centre again. Albert Einstein famously said, 'We cannot solve our problems with the same thinking we used when we created them.' That's what this intentional period of non-deciding offers us. It creates an opportunity to reset before we go again. What I know to be true is that we're naturally more decisive when we don't feel the pressure to respond immediately. We're wiser when we create a framework to make decisions. So that thing that your mind is looping on, make a decision today to not decide on it for a specific time period. That might be a day, a few days or a week. Then, set the intention that you'll know better what your next right step is as you emerge from your period of non-deciding.

PART 2 - SOWING THE SEEDS

# Obstacles or detours

With hindsight, it's easy to connect the dots and to understand why things played out the way they did at particular times in our life. We need to remind ourselves today that when things feel a little off track, we'll look back not too far from now and be able to make sense of what's unfolding. When we journey a little further, we'll be able to see the gifts of our circumstances.

When I experience hesitation or a feeling of being lost or stuck when things don't quite go as planned, this line from author and spiritual teacher Gabrielle Bernstein always helps to soothe my anxiety and to strengthen my trust: 'Obstacles are detours in the right direction.'

When I look back and thread together my past experiences, the things that didn't go exactly as I'd hoped they would were simply guiding me towards something that was more aligned, better, more fulfilling, deeper and richer.

What if the plan that you have for yourself is only 10 per cent of what's possible for you? When we can hold this idea and trust that any obstacles that appear on our path are simply guiding us in the *right* direction, there are no roadblocks. These detours are navigating us on another path that's going to be *more* joyful, *more* adventurous, *more* magical and filled with *more* wonder, *more* delight and *more* awe than we could've possibly imagined for ourselves.

When we look at our life through this lens, we wake up to the experience that's in front of us, in this moment, and cultivate the energy of eager anticipation of the unfolding journey. We can get out of our own way and trust that there's a loving influence guiding us towards what we want, in ways that are bigger, bolder and more magical than we could've envisaged for ourselves.

**Ask yourself:**
- Where are the perceived obstacles in my life right now?
- What's something that didn't go as planned?
- How might this have actually been part of the plan?

Perhaps it's the relationship that didn't go as you'd hoped, the client you didn't sign or the job you didn't get. How could those potential obstacles have been detours in the *right* direction? Sit with that potential today. Write about it in your journal. What lies ahead is so much richer than what you had planned for yourself.

PART 2 - SOWING THE SEEDS

# Rubber Balls

Modern life can mean that we regularly feel like we have a lot of balls in the air at any one time. Family, work, health, exercise, travel, study, oh and sleep… (if we can get enough of it!). We can often have a lot of things going on and it can feel overwhelming, exhausting and endless.

I heard an author of a bestselling book on productivity and success ('success' by career standards, that is) declare recently in an interview, 'We must never drop a ball!'

It was based around this idea that we have to ensure that every. single. ball. we're juggling is to be taken care of and in motion at all times. I disagree wholeheartedly.

This extreme grit and determination may be sustainable in the short term, but we can't possibly live a full and balanced life with this intense pressure applied to us consistently and without rest. Different seasons of our life will have us prioritising different areas of our life. For example, when my sons were little, they were my top priority, so my business and my exercise routine took a back seat. As my sons got older, I was able to prioritise my work more because they were at school for six-and-a-half hours every day.

These different seasons, these different phases of our life, will have us prioritising different aspects of who we are. I want to offer you a practice to really help you discern what your priorities are today, so you don't risk slipping into overwhelm.

Take a piece of paper and write down all that you have to do today. All of those balls that are in the air, write them down on the page. Then, I want you to categorise these balls that you have in the air as either Glass Balls or Rubber Balls.

We want to make sure that we tend to those Glass Balls—those are the things that if we drop them, they will hit the floor and smash. We know what areas of our life are Glass Balls. These are things that are really important to our heart and we want to give them the care, nurturance and attention that they need and deserve in this phase of our life. What you'll discover in this practice is that these Glass Balls are actually very few in number.

Next, I want you to identify the balls you have in the air that are in fact Rubber Balls. When they're Rubber Balls, it means that we're allowed to let them fall. They're allowed to hit the ground because they won't smash. They'll simply bounce right back up when we have the capacity to hold them in a greater way.

**Ask yourself:**
- What are my Glass Balls?
- What are my Rubber Balls?

PART 2 - SOWING THE SEEDS

# Considering the opposite

A quote by Gay Hendricks, from his brilliant book *The Big Leap*: 'Each of us has an inner thermostat setting that determines how much love, success and creativity we allow ourselves to enjoy. When we exceed our inner thermostat setting, we will often do something to sabotage ourselves, causing us to drop back into the old, familiar zone where we feel secure.'

There were years where I can now see that I held myself back from achieving the goals that I told myself were important to me. I can see this most clearly through the goals that I held for my business. I had goals of wanting to achieve financial stability, to make a positive contribution and to be of service in a deep and meaningful way. But underneath these goals, I could see there were some things that were unconsciously holding me back from taking the inspired action required to create opportunities for these goals to be fulfilled.

These were beliefs such as: *If I earn more money, I'll need to deal with more complicated financial stuff.* I didn't believe I was capable of dealing with finance at that level of business. I also had this belief: *More exposure would equal more criticism.* That is, if I were to be more visible in my work and in the world, then I'd be vulnerable to people's judgement and criticism. This was another belief that really held me back from moving towards these goals: *The more successful I am in my business, the more time it will take away from me to spend with my kids.*

This last belief was a really big one for me, because I wanted to have a successful business, I wanted to do really meaningful work and make an impact in the world, but I also wanted to be a present parent. I wanted to be able to be there for my kids, to be able to spend quality time with them—especially in the years before they went to school.

In my mind, I equated success with me being away from home more and having to potentially travel with work. These were things that ultimately held me back and stopped me taking the action that I was being inspired to take, which created an oppositional tide of energy within me.

This notion of either being the parent who created the financial prosperity in the family or being the parent who was present and available was something that stemmed from my own childhood.

My dad ran his own business, which took up a lot of his time, energy and attention, especially when my siblings and I were little, so it was my mum that was at home with us kids. She would be there before school. She would be there when we got home from school. She would take us to our sporting activities. She would be there to make dinner.

Because of this experience, I cultivated the belief that you were either the absent, earning parent *or* the present, loving parent. It has taken me some time to untangle these beliefs.

**Ask yourself:**
**What are the negative implications of me getting everything I want?**

When you think of those seeds you have sown for yourself, what are the perceived negative implications that you believe you'll have to experience if those seeds take root and bloom?

**What would I have to give up if I achieve that goal?**

In my example, for me to have achieved the goal of the business success that I wanted to create, I believed that I'd have to give up time with my kids. So, that was the payoff for me. It was either to have a successful business and give up time with my kids, or give up on the business and spend time with my kids.

**What if the opposite were true?**

I perceived that having a financially successful business would mean that I'd have to deal with more complicated financial matters. But what if the opposite were true? What if earning more money made the finances more simple? What if it gave me the opportunity and resources to bring someone into my team to help me navigate those matters, which ultimately made things more simple and less complicated?

With my belief of more exposure equalling more criticism, what if the opposite were true? What if more exposure didn't equal more criticism? What if more exposure actually equalled more impact, more influence, more service, more contribution?

With my belief that business success would result in time away from my kids, what if the opposite were true of that too? What if the more successful my business became, the more time I had to spend with my kids?

All of these opposites are actually things that have come true for me in my business, by simply taking these limiting, self-sabotaging beliefs, and flipping them on their head. Where can you flip the script of your own habitual stories? Where are you holding on to stories and beliefs that are causing you hurt? What would courage suggest?

PART 2 - SOWING THE SEEDS

# Stillness moves mountains

*'If a problem looks difficult, relax. If it looks impossible, relax even more. Then begin encouraging small changes, putting just enough pressure on yourself to move one turtle step forward. Then rest, savour, celebrate. Then step again. You'll find that slow is fast, gentle is powerful and stillness moves mountains.'*
— Martha Beck

We can often feel like we need to be taking giant, significant leaps each and every day towards the life that we desire the most. But as humans, we're unable to sustain this level of output with consistency. What's more important is to be consistent in a sustainable way, because taking small, consistent steps creates magic in our lives.

It can feel insignificant on any particular day, but the compound effect of small steps taken consistently is what creates magic. We don't have to know what to do next month or next year. All we have to do is focus on what's right in front of us today.

With my clients, I use a structure of getting them to set a 90 Day Goal—a ninety-day intention of what they want to create in the world.

This ninety-day period is the sweet spot between giving ourselves enough time to create something new that doesn't exist yet, but it's also short enough that we feel motivated to take action tomorrow and in the immediate future. We shouldn't know exactly what we need to do on every day from Day 1. The way that I like to structure this with my clients is that we set the intention for Day 90, and we make a plan towards that. But that plan is flexible, malleable. We check in on Day 30 and Day 60 so that we can readjust and recalibrate as a result of what we've learned along the way.

If we're trying to create something that doesn't exist yet, we're going to have to learn new skills, show up in different ways, take a lot of inspired action and be willing to fail, make some course corrections and go again.

When we're on the hamster wheel of life and we're hustling and trying to take massive action each and every day, it results in burnout, overwhelm and exhaustion, which is when we give up. So, how can we make it more sustainable? We need to allow for more ease on our way towards creating those goals we've set the intention for. We must move slowly and gently and see the value of stillness.

Stillness lets us hear our own thoughts. It lets us witness our own ideas. It allows us to offer ourselves the answers, rather than looking outside of ourselves for the answers. It guides us towards inspiration about what to do next.

## PART 2 - SOWING THE SEEDS

I invite you to carve out ten minutes today to allow yourself to sit in stillness. Allow yourself to hear your thoughts, recognise those ideas and develop answers for some of those questions you might have.

These ten minutes may be when you're in your car, when you get home from work, in the morning while you wait for your coffee to brew or while the kids are doing their homework or watching TV.

Ten minutes a day over the course of a month equates to five hours. How might your life be different if you listened to your own thoughts in stillness for five hours over the next month? It can be all too easy to convince ourselves that we don't have this spare time. But what if spending these ten minutes in stillness each day allowed you to know what to do next with more clarity, assuredness and certainty?

As author Martha Beck says, 'slow is fast, gentle is powerful and stillness moves mountains'.

PART 2 - SOWING THE SEEDS

# The antidote to frustration

I recently had a day where the juggle of parenthood and work had me ready to lock myself in my bedroom and not leave for a considerable amount of time. This was a bitter pill to swallow.

Yes, I spend my days coaching clients on how to balance work and family life, but I'm also human and not immune to getting looped into negative self-talk at times.

As I sat on my bed while my kids watched Netflix in the living room, I pulled out my journal and started free writing about all the things my boys were doing that were pissing me off. It was a long list, but here's a little snippet of what was on there:

- *They're so impatient with each other.*
- *They never listen.*
- *They're forever changing their minds.*
- *They never give me a second.*
- *They're so disorganised.*
- *They've got no attention span.*
- *They're wasteful with food.*
- *They forget to tell me things until the last minute.*
- *They constantly interrupt me.*

Now, none of this is new, right? If you're a parent, you can probably relate to every one of these frustrations.

Here's why writing them down was so helpful. When we have a judgement or frustration with someone else, it's almost always a judgement or frustration we have within ourselves. I know this intellectually, but in the height of the frustration, I sure as hell didn't want to accept it. Nevertheless, I knew it was true. So, I rewrote the list replacing 'they' with 'I'.

- *I'm so impatient.*
- *I never listen.*
- *I'm forever changing my mind.*
- *I never give myself a second.*
- *I'm so disorganised.*
- *I've got no attention span.*
- *I'm wasteful.*
- *I forget things until the last minute.*
- *I'm constantly interrupting them.*

This is what's really going on. Yes, some frustrations were warranted. (I really do wish Noah would put his dirty socks in the laundry basket, which isn't a projection of my own frustration!) But nine times out of ten, the things we wish other people would do are actually the things we wish we would do.

Get curious. Who's pissing you off today? Write a list. Then, circle the ones that are true about you. Practising self-compassion, gentle acceptance and acknowledgement that no-one's perfect brings us closer to those we love and closer to ourselves. It's in our willingness to be vulnerable that we see the truth and purity of our humanness.

PART 2 - SOWING THE SEEDS

# Slow your pace, unleash your joy

How do you describe your day when someone asks you? Busy? Hectic? Crazy?

We can easily default to these ways of describing what's unfolded throughout our day. It's often an unconscious, knee-jerk response. Even on days where we actually don't have so much on our schedule, we don't give ourselves permission to announce to others that we have a quiet day. It feels lazy and unproductive, insignificant and self-indulgent.

I've noticed that while we exhaustedly fly the flag of over-doing, at the same time we stifle our expression of joy and enthusiasm. It all goes towards helping us fit in, to be relatable and in sync with those around us. It's bitterly uncommon to communicate our un-busyness and our excitement to others.

The modus operandi of our modern society is doubly negative—a resignation to endless checklist ticking, coupled with a meek appetite for indifference.

But this isn't where we'll find magic, wonder or awe that's waiting to be discovered. We must give ourselves permission to express our natural delight that bubbles just under the surface. We need to allow, at times, what simmers to boil over. We see children do it all the time—an effervescence they don't think to temper. This allowance of joy is contagious; as we loosen up the stagnant energy and express ourselves more fully, it invites others to do the same. It gives them permission to unlock the playfulness and the excitable within them.

**Ask yourself:**
- Where can I unleash some joy today?
- In what ways can I express more playfulness?
- What's asking to be unlocked within me?

PART 2 - SOWING THE SEEDS

# Having no opinion

There's immense freedom in having no opinion. You might need to be reminded of this—I know I do on a regular basis—but you don't have to have an opinion on everything.

Often, we're scared to not have an opinion on something. We're scared that we'll look uneducated, stupid, uncaring or unkind for not knowing about something and not having a strong opinion on it.

Taking the stance of non-opinion can be most liberating. Someone can care deeply about something that's completely irrelevant to you. Someone can be incredibly offended by a particular comment that doesn't even register with you.

This isn't about being uncaring or being without compassion for the suffering in the world. But we can't take on a 10/10 level of interest on every single issue and subject. There are a whole lot of things—both big and small—that we can choose to simply have no opinion on.

It's the most authentic approach we can take— to not pretend to know or to care about something, but to lovingly and honestly communicate our lack of knowledge or our lack of passion on a particular subject.

It's an act of deep integrity and confidence that frees us and allows us to funnel more of our love, energy and attention into the things, circumstances, events and people that we actually do really care about.

**Ask yourself:**
- What are three things I can choose to simply have no opinion on today?

These might be things in conversations at work. These might be things in conversations with your partner. These might be things in conversations with your mum or your dad or your kid. Where can you lovingly hold that space of non-opinion?

As Stoic philosopher Marcus Aurelius says in his book *Meditations*: 'We have the power to hold no opinion about a thing and to not let it upset our state of mind—for things have no natural power to shape our judgements.'

PART 2 - SOWING THE SEEDS

# Barely at 10 per cent

Overwhelmed, over-extended, over-committed… These habitual ways of being in the world can make us feel like we need to opt out for a while, to say 'yes' less and 'no' more. It feels true to us, so we believe that we must retreat into ourselves, excavate all that feels stuck and bothersome in order for us to know what we must reorganise and reprioritise in our lives.

What I know to be true is that while there are seasons for such retreat, the time required of us in this place is far shorter and less frequent than we allow ourselves to indulge in. We call it exhaustion and depletion. But what we actually discover, when we look under the crust that has formed over our lives, is a boredom, a frustration. Inertia is cunning and can disguise herself convincingly as overwhelm.

We tell ourselves that we need to do less, but what if the antidote to this uncreative way of being is to actually do more?

We have a tendency to believe that we're operating constantly at 90 per cent of our capacity. This can be born out of habit and influenced by our always on, always busy culture. But there's an alternative. How would your life be different if you viewed your current contribution as barely 10 per cent of what you're capable of? What if you had way more to give yourself and others than you've been believing? I'm not suggesting that we burn ourselves out or mindlessly expend our personal resources, but rather be open to the possibility that we, in fact, have vast tanks of resources that are currently untapped.

You're not overwhelmed, you're bored. You're not burnt out, you're a fading flicker. You're not doing too much, you're doing too little. What if you turned the tide of your life? What if you decided to view it not as something that was dying, but impatiently waiting to be born? What if this bone-deep exhaustion is because of your withholding? How would you move through this day, this week, this month, if you believed that the replenishment you crave would meet you one step forward from where you currently are, not one step back?

PART 2 - SOWING THE SEEDS

# Simple loves

We spend a disproportionate amount of time focusing on what's missing and what's wrong, and not nearly enough time celebrating all that's here and right. The simple loves that we experience can bring us the most tender and liberating joy. Here are some of my simple loves:

**I love** seeing a text message from my son appear on my phone. It's a reminder of how small things grow slowly, then all of a sudden. **I love** the middle day of a long weekend away, where you get to wake up and fall asleep in the new place just once. **I love** scanning the bookshelves of homes I visit. You can learn a lot about the people who live there through their library. **I love** people who laugh easily and loudly. **I love** watching my sons stare out the window on long car journeys, their hearts and minds in far-off places I'll never know fully. **I love** waking up a few minutes before the alarm goes off. There's stillness and quiet, with nothing to call my attention from myself. **I love** the feeling of sand on the floor of our home. It's a beautiful reminder of the water close by. **I love** coupling together what little is in the fridge for dinner. It feels like both resourcefulness and ease. **I love** how music can crack open even the most armoured of hearts. **I love** the feeling of seeing something funny and knowing the exact person to send it to. Shared humour is an indication of true soul friendship. **I love** watching my sons play sports and them also watching me. It dissolves hierarchy and lets us see one another in a different light. **I love** doing nothing much with people I love dearly. **I love** the brief and regular pockets of presence available in the few minutes it takes for the kettle to boil when making a cup of tea. This is my only form of multitasking. **I love** the golden snippets my youngest son shares about his day, right as I'm about to switch off his bedroom light. I feel the importance and safety these late-night moments will hold as he grows. **I love** knowing that at the end of a particularly challenging day, tomorrow is a fresh page. **I love** knowing the sun is always there, even on the days I can't see it or feel it. Weather is fleetingly inconsistent; a gentle reminder to resource my life from that which is vibrant, bright and always available.

**Ask yourself:**
- What simple loves are present in my life today?
- What are three things that are available for me to appreciate exactly as they are today?
- What do I love to hear, to smell, to taste, to see and to touch?

PART 2 - SOWING THE SEEDS

# **More**

The seductive and addictive lure of more. It's natural to want more. As humans, we're wired to search for what's next. It's aided our survival for thousands of years, but today, in our modern society, we can have more of most things at the tap of an app or click of a mouse.

It's not exclusively selfish to want more. Oftentimes, we want more of something for those we love. For example:

- More time *for* our kids.
- More money *for* the causes and conscious businesses we want to support.
- More patience *for* our partner.
- More forgiveness *for* our parents.
- More focus *for* our work.

When it comes to the wanting of more, we can split them into two categories:

- More of what we already have.
- More of something new.

The 'more of what we already have' is when we turn up the volume on the aspects that already exist in our lives. Slightly more money each month, a little more free time at the weekends, a shade more focus for the work we're engaged in. This is the 'more' that most of us default to. We take what we have and try to make it bigger.

But instead, what if the 'more' you created was more newness, more novelty, more diversity, more scope, more breadth, more texture, more experiences, more of what's currently unseen?

It's tricky for our brains to grasp this, because we're not in the habit of considering what we can't see in front of us.

**Ask yourself:**
- What 'more' could I weave into my life that would give me more breadth of experience, not just more of the same?

PART 2 - SOWING THE SEEDS

# Lists

My journal is more a collection of lists than anything else. I'm not a fan of to-do lists or checklists but, somehow, using the structure of lists invokes a magical power in helping us understand our thoughts. Here are the types of lists I find most helpful:

**Lists of appreciation that help me shift my energy from lack and frustration to abundance and gratitude.**
For example:
- Lists of things to appreciate.
- Lists of the things and people I love.
- Lists of things I'm grateful for.

These lists contain things from the epic and obvious (my sons, my privilege as a free woman living in Australia, the fresh water that runs through my taps) to the tiny and delightful (the sunny spot I share with my dog in the morning as I meditate, the smell of coffee brewing in the morning before my boys wake, the smile of a stranger in a car as I let them pass).

**Lists that help me understand the mix of emotions that are asking for attention within me.**

For example:
- List of things that might be causing me to feel unsettled.
- List of things I'm currently scared about.
- List of questions I want to ask but I feel frightened of the answers.
- List of all the ways something could dramatically fail.

**Lists that help me understand what my right next step should be.**

For example:
- List of ideas that excite me.
- List of potential wonderful outcomes.
- List of all the ways I might feel joyful today.
- List of ways this particular, hard-seeming thing could be simple and easy.

**Lists that help me find my knowing.**

These are the 'pros versus cons' lists that you might have used at some point. I write a list of all the reasons why Option A is a good idea, and then a list of all the reasons why Option B is a good idea. The purpose of this list is not about choosing based on logic. Oftentimes, Option A will have twenty items and Option B will have two, and I'll choose Option B.

PART 2 - SOWING THE SEEDS

This style of list lets us access our hearts. It allows us to drop down from our busy heads and to move through life in a more heart-minded way.

I invite you to write some lists today. Use any of my suggestions or come up with your own. Lists provide us with clarity, insight, knowing and, most of all, peace.

PART 2 - SOWING THE SEEDS

# Living beyond twenty-three

In the business world, there's a lot of talk about finding your niche. Be the one who finds a specific answer to a very specific problem. For some, this is clarifying and generates focus. For others, it's stifling and generates resentment. I believe the same is true in life, not just business.

Much of what we need to learn in order to navigate life successfully and safely is acquired by the time we're aged twenty-three. So, it makes logical sense that we would stop striving for more information by that age. We find our niche—our sweet and comfy spot—and then we 'do life'. We climb the ladder, accumulate the things, buy and sell a few homes, perhaps grow our family.

But what about *us*? What part do we play in this life? What about our creativity, our contribution, our passions, our sense of self? Unless we make the intentional choice to grow and mature our hearts past twenty-three, we create more of the same. We sit in the well-worn grooves of the niche we've carved out for ourselves. By twenty-three, we know how to survive, but do we know how to thrive?

We're creatures of habit; we like familiarity and the known. But is that a life experienced fully or simply a life witnessed passively? What if we allowed ourselves to explore, to navigate new ways of showing up in the world? What if we tapped into inspiration and followed the sparks? What if we invited more wonder, more learning? What if, rather than more continuing of the known, we opted for more beginning of what's new?

# Three alternative realities

We know all about the power of visualisation and the magic a good ol' vision board can conjure, but the downside of being super prescriptive about exactly *how* we'd like our lives to unfold is that it leaves us with a 'win or lose' result.

We either get everything we want, or close to everything, and we feel like we're winning, that we're being intentional creators of our lives. Or, we don't get all we've pinned and stuck to that vision board, and we feel like we've failed.

I want to offer you the possibility of there being an endless number of realities you *could* live that would feel like success. Give this exercise a go…

Get three individual pieces of paper and, on each, answer the following questions for three wildly different potential lives you could live. The first might be the one that's most familiar to you—the one that you have the most focus and attention on now. Then, I want you to come up with two vastly different alternatives to that 'perfect' scenario.

- Who do I live with?
- Where do I live?
- What do I see when I look out the window?

- What do I do for work?
- Who do I work with?
- What communities am I connected with?
- What projects and causes get me fired up and excited?
- Where and with whom will I spend next Christmas or my next birthday?
- Who is the last person I called or texted?

This journalling exercise is so powerful as it cracks us open to more breadth, more novelty, more adventure, more texture than we often allow ourselves to experience. It allows us to embody wonder, curiosity, fascination and eager expectation of delightful things unfolding.

Hold a vision of how you want to feel (for me right now, my North Star emotions are contribution, intimacy, joy and peace), and then go out into the world and allow people, places, experiences and opportunities that are aligned with these emotions to magnetise themselves to you, and draw you towards them.

# Tend to your corner of the garden

Impact, contribution, influence… We can feel like these are out of reach unless we are bestselling authors, leaders of countries or with endless financial resources to facilitate change. This limited thinking causes us to freeze and feel helpless. We feel like our value is inferior in comparison. But the truth is, we're not all supposed to be top of *The New York Times* bestseller list, president of a nation or a billionaire.

That said, if these *are* desires of yours—if the idea of this stokes a fire in your belly—then by all means go right ahead, follow that desire, set the intention and move in that direction each day. But many of us are capable of making incredible contributions and creating ripples of wonder across the globe by tending to our 'corner of the garden' as author, speaker and politician Marianne Williamson puts it.

**Ask yourself:**
- How can I tend to my 'corner of the garden' today?

Here are some ideas:

**Be open to courageous and vulnerable conversions.**

If these are with your partner, for example, it might create a new example for your kids on how to navigate conflict. Or perhaps you inspire an onlooker to be bolder and more courageous themselves.

**Check in on an elderly neighbour.**

By sharing a cup of tea and asking them about their life, it might give them the lift they need, help them feel more relevant and give them confidence to re-engage in activities they've let slip over the past few years.

**Set boundaries for the entire household around technology.**

Perhaps you all charge your phones in the kitchen at night and agree to no screens at the table during dinner—this might provide daily pockets of connection for kids to feel safe to share things about their life and what's going on for them, and also shred any potential hierarchical dynamic of one rule for kids, another for adults. (Because we actually don't really need our phones for an alarm, or to reply to that one email during dinner. I'm speaking from recent experience with this one!)

PART 2 - SOWING THE SEEDS

**Also ask yourself:**
- Who lives in or regularly visits my 'corner of the garden'?
- How can I tend to these relationships in meaningful ways?

I feel a bubbling sense of optimism for our world when I imagine what would happen if we all tended to our own 'corner of the garden'.

# Part 3
# Allowing to bloom

*To allow… to receive… to surrender… to stop holding back… to release resistance… to feel worthy of… to expect… to go with the flow… to welcome with wonder and awe*

On the surface, this seems like the easiest and most passive part of the process. But in my own experience and in the experiences of many of my clients, this is actually where we become stuck.

We've tilled the soil and prepared the ground, we've sowed the seeds of intention to design and cultivate the life we most want to live, and now we have to relax and allow it to bloom. The reason that this is so difficult for many of us is because we're conditioned to believe that in order to create anything of any value in our lives, we must shed our blood, sweat and tears to attain it. It's true, hustle and persistent action *will* garner results, and so it's logical to think that if we want more results we must simply try harder. Effort in = results out. But this is where we've departed from the truth of how life actually unfolds.

This part asks us to muster the greatest courage of all: to have faith in that which we can't see yet. When we define what we want and set our intentions, regardless of whether that's aloud to another person or silently in the pages of our journal, the wheels are already set in motion. Our job now is to allow it to come into our conscious awareness. Let me be clear… this is not magical thinking or simply hoping and wishing for something to happen. It's a relinquishing of the control we've been naively taught to foster in order to create the life we want to live. It's not to say that there's no action required in this part, but we must connect to our heart and get into alignment in order to receive the inspiration to take a particular action. Our overly logical minds struggle with this. Logic calls for a five-step action plan, a checklist, a clearly signposted path from basecamp to summit. Yet, when we reflect, very few of the wonderful things, people, opportunities and places we've journeyed through have followed this sensible, methodical and essentially uncreative path.

Allowing the seeds we've planted to take root and begin to bloom takes time. This is the invisible work we can't see happening under the surface. We have faith that the literal seeds we plant in our garden will sprout when they're strong enough, and we must borrow this same faith and allowing for the less-tangible-but-no-less-real seeds planted in our lives. This isn't easy for us. We've become so expectant of instantaneous blooming that it's unbearably painful for us to have to wait for the gestation of what we want to come to fruition.

We have the choice: to view life as working with us, together, side by side, or against us, as something we have to overcome and defeat.

Controlling says, *I'll make this happen because I want it.* Allowing says, *I'll let this unfold if it's meant for me.*

When I made the decision to allow myself to be guided by something other than my analytical, logical mind, my days began to fill with wonder, awe and delight. The iron grip I'd had on my life had cut me off from noticing the magic and synchronicity that was all around me. It'd been there all along, but I hadn't been available to it. I was unable to see it or feel it.

Allowing comes down to trust. Trust that what we want also wants us. Trust that we're worthy of our desires. Trust that all is well, that everything is unfolding for us and that we're guided and supported, even when we feel lost and alone on our path at times.

Our joy is not reserved for when the flowers have finally bloomed or when the ripe fruit is ready to be picked and eaten, for there's abundant satisfaction in witnessing the process of becoming. The notes that lie ahead will help you to get in sync with the gentle, slow and natural gestation of the seeds you have sown. Time takes on a different texture when you allow this blooming to occur.

It may look like you're doing less, yet more seems to be unfolding on your path. This is the magic of allowing. When we gently place down the oars we've been tirelessly paddling upstream with, we allow ourselves to be taken on a downstream adventure, where everything we've set the intention for is waiting to meet us. Let's begin.

PART 3 - ALLOWING TO BLOOM

# Swapping having for being

Often we want to have a particular thing, to have a particular result. But we don't give enough attention to what it will feel like to be in that result, to be in that particular situation.

Let me give you a couple of examples:
- *Having* a baby versus *being* a parent.
- *Having* clients versus *being* of service to people.
- *Having* a wedding versus *being* committed to a person.
- *Having* the ultimate beach body versus *being* strong, healthy and vibrant.

I encourage you to write down a list of all the things that you want to have. Then ask yourself, What do I imagine I'll feel when I have that?

The reason we want anything—whether it's the relationship, the money, the house, the car, the trip—is because of how we imagine we'll *feel* when we have it. So, rather than wanting those external things, and the 'having' energy of them, how can you transform that into the 'being' energy? There's much more momentum in that energy of being versus the materialistic energy of having.

**Ask yourself:**
- What are all the things that I want to have?
- How do I imagine I'll feel when I have those things?
- How can I embody those feelings, those beings, in some small way today?

PART 3 - ALLOWING TO BLOOM

# Cultivating our own wisdom

Author and neuroscientist Dr Joe Dispenza says 'a memory without the emotional charge is called wisdom', which means that our past experiences can hold some of our deepest wisdom. But when we hold on hungrily to the painful emotions from these past experiences, it can block us from cultivating, and consequently sharing, this wisdom.

Times where I've been able to access my own wisdom were when I became a mother for the first time, and when I was completing my marriage and navigating divorce. These lived experiences allow me to offer my wisdom to friends, clients and family members who might find themselves in similar situations. But when people are so deeply entrenched in their current experiences, they're not able to access the wisdom because of the intensity and flooding of emotion.

I can look back now on the experience of getting a divorce and I can look back now on the experience of being a new mother and access some of the wisdom from these experiences because, from this vantage point, I'm not so intrinsically held to the emotions of those past experiences.

**Ask yourself:**
- What past experiences can I cultivate wisdom from?
- Where am I holding on to an emotion from the past that's holding me back from wisdom that's available to me?
- How can I retell some of those stories from the past in ways that are for me, not against me?
- What ways can I really help myself move forwards rather than keeping myself stuck in the past?

Wisdom comes from those past experiences where the emotional charge has dissolved. You have the ability to cultivate wisdom from those past experiences.

So, spend some time reflecting and see where you can cultivate your own wisdom that you can share with yourself today, with your future self and with your loved ones.

PART 3 - ALLOWING TO BLOOM

# Magnetism

There's a reciprocity to magnetism. We're taught in the personal-development world that humans are magnetic and that we need to line up with the things that we want to create in order for them to be magnetised to us, but this is only part of the equation.

Artist Pablo Picasso summed it up perfectly when he said, 'Inspiration exists, but it has to find you working.' I love this idea that it's a two-way exchange. Being magnetic isn't about being passive and waiting exclusively for things to be magnetised to us. It also requires us to take inspired action—to be willing and curious about what's around the corner and to be agile and engaged with the world, our creativity and our imagination—by allowing ourselves to also be magnetised *to other things*. This is what I take the 'find you working' phrase of the quote to mean.

We shouldn't be hustling, overworking and stressing ourselves out in this endless quest to achieve all. the. things. But, we have to be willing to take inspired action. Often that notion of inspired action doesn't make logical sense in the moment. It might be something simple, such as being inspired to go to a different cafe for your morning coffee, to drive a different route to work, to take a different class at the gym.

The expectation of being a stationary being that waits only for things, people and opportunities to be magnetised to us goes against the nature of reciprocity. It stops us from going out there and putting ourselves in front of opportunities, situations and experiences that could create more of what we want. We have to allow ourselves to be drawn to these things.

A great example of this is with one of my dear friends who was happily single a few years ago. She wasn't looking for a relationship, but she was definitely open to it. She'd been invited to a party at a friend's place and she really didn't want to go, but there was this niggling little spark inside her that told her perhaps she *should* go.

So, she went along to the party and got chatting to a guy who is now her long-term partner who she has a home with, who she's created a family with. She speaks to this idea of allowing herself to be magnetised to that party. It's not about sitting at home waiting for someone to come and knock on the door. When we get our energy right, we take the inspired action, we allow for magic, we allow for synchronicity, we allow for a chance to happen.

We have to be out in the world to be available to chance. The inspiration happens, but we have to take the action. The Universe can't take action for us. It can simply offer us that invitational spark of inspiration, and then we have to follow through with the action. We don't have to know the reason, but we do need to get out of our own way at times.

PART 3 - ALLOWING TO BLOOM

    The Universe is lining up these opportunities for us all the time, but if it doesn't look exactly how we thought it *should* look, we're quick to dismiss it. Allow things to be magnetised *to you* and also *you to them*. It's time to meet the Universe halfway.

PART 3 - ALLOWING TO BLOOM

# Broaden out in all directions

Popular goal-setting advice would have us get very specific on an area of our life, and then go all in on that one thing. Or, perhaps it might be that we want to cover all of our bases, so we're encouraged to pick three areas—work, health, relationships—get very specific on what we want to achieve in each of these three areas, and again go all in. Laser focus, single-mindedness, grit, determination, all-or-nothing energy. I, too, used to believe that this was the way to achieve what I ultimately wanted.

Yes, a defined goal creates focus and helps us generate momentum in a specific direction, but the flip side is that we can become very conditional and prescriptive about the *how* and the *when* around this particular goal or set of goals.

When we set goals, it's not the actual goal we crave, but the feeling that we imagine we'll feel when we've achieved the goal. That's what we *actually* want.

Let me give you a few examples:
- **We want to earn more money.** The reason we want to earn more money is because we want to feel that sense of security, of abundance, of financial certainty and safety.

- **We want to find the perfect partner or improve our relationship with our current partner.** The reason we want this is because we imagine the sense of intimacy, connection and commitment that we'll feel from having achieved that goal.

- **We want to work three days a week.** The reason we want to do this is because we imagine that in doing so, we'll have more balance, more time to rest, more time with our family, more time to exercise, more time to be spontaneous.

- **We want to write a bestselling book.** We don't really want the physical book on the shelf. What we really want is that sense of contribution, of creativity, of collaboration, of working with a team to produce the book and have it published and be out there in the world.

The reason that we want what we want is because of how we imagine we'll feel when we've achieved that. When we believe that we need something to feel a particular way, we're doing life back-to-front. It puts so much pressure on particular areas of our life to have us feel a particular way. We don't want to put the pressure of intimacy on a relationship, for example. There are other ways that we can experience that feeling of intimacy outside of our immediate relationships.

When we focus on one thing that we don't have yet, what we're actually doing is putting attention on the lack of it, and all that does is push it further and further away from us.

So, rather than trying to 'fix' an area of your life, where can you find ease to appreciate and cultivate that emotion in other ways? Here's an example in the context of intimacy:

- Where can I cultivate a sense of intimacy separate from my relationship?
- Where can I cultivate a sense of intimacy in my work?
- Where can I cultivate a sense of intimacy with myself?
- Where can I cultivate a sense of intimacy at home, with my family?
- Where can I cultivate a sense of intimacy in my life through exercise and eating?

There are lots of different ways that we can cultivate something without putting the pressure on that one area, that one person, that one goal of our life. We want to broaden our lives in all directions and be less conditional about how exactly we experience the emotions we desire.

**Ask yourself:**
- **What is it that I want?**

Write down what you want to create or achieve, then ask yourself…

- **How do I imagine I'll feel when I get that, when I become that or when I create that?**

Once we know that feeling underneath the goal, we can then get creative about how we can experience that feeling. Then, once you've identified what the feeling underneath the goal is, ask yourself:

- **How can I experience this feeling in some capacity today?**

This isn't to stop you from wanting to achieve the goals and dreams that you have for yourself in your life, but when we can take the pressure off that specific thing, person or outcome to give us those emotions, we're far more likely to realise our intentions.

So, broaden out in all directions. Don't get caught up in the minute details of *how* or *when*. Instead, create as many opportunities as possible to make yourself available to those feelings. How can you make yourself available to intimacy today? How can you make yourself available to abundance, to connection, to peace, to prosperity, to joy? Then, open yourself to being delighted by how it unfolds in your day.

PART 3 - ALLOWING TO BLOOM

# Guilt versus shame

I'd like to explore the difference between guilt and shame. Author Brené Brown has such a beautiful definition of these two emotions: Guilt is, 'I did something bad.' Shame is, 'I am bad.'

This subtle distinction is incredibly important to recognise, especially when it comes to conversations that we're having with our children. Here's a story from my own life where this has played out.

My son came home from school and gave me a note. Before I read the note, he told me what it was about. He said that there were some kids in his class who had vandalised some furniture in the classroom. When the teacher had realised this, he sat down the class and asked them all to write on a sticky note the name of someone that they knew was responsible for this vandalising. The teacher then collected the notes—some of which were blank, some had names on them—and went through the notes to identify who was responsible. My son's name came out as one of the people responsible.

The people responsible had to write a letter to their parents explaining what had happened, to really acknowledge that they were aware of what they'd done and to offer their sincere apologies.

When I read the note he had written for me, I realised I had this beautiful opportunity to acknowledge where shame and guilt could potentially be present. This idea of shame being 'I am wrong' and guilt being 'I did something wrong' was going to be really important to this conversation. I wanted him to know that he didn't have to feel shame for this. He wasn't broken or less than as a human because of this action that he'd chosen to take. Yes, it was wrong to take that action—he did something wrong—but he, as a person, was not wrong or broken.

It's so important for our children to realise that they're not broken as humans, they're not ultimately flawed. Yes, they're going to mess up, they're going to follow the crowd and do things that they most likely know are wrong. As children, they can get caught up in a group and act in ways that they know aren't how they want to show up in the world.

This conversation enabled us to connect in a deep and meaningful way, and let me assure him that it's okay to mess up—it's okay to do something wrong—but it's important that we show up with integrity. This way, we can be honest and acknowledge that we did something wrong but without feeling that we're intrinsically broken.

Through our conversation, I realised that he had in fact written his own name on the sticky note. He had volunteered his wrongdoing to the teacher and was willing to face the consequences that were going to be served up.

PART 3 - ALLOWING TO BLOOM

In that moment, I'd never been prouder of my son—knowing that he didn't wait to be found out, that he volunteered himself knowing that he was in the wrong.

It's so easy to be reactionary, to yell, to shout, to blame, to make people wrong, to deal out consequences and punishments in the moment. But I saw my son's humaneness and let him know that it's okay to mess up. I said to him: 'This is going to happen throughout your whole life. But what can you learn from this particular situation? Perhaps it's to give yourself a little pause. Perhaps it's to not always follow the crowd. Perhaps it's to tune in and make a slightly better decision than the one you previously made.'

This experience allowed me to see my son as separate from me, and know that his wrongdoing isn't a reflection on me as a parent. Him having the confidence to come and speak to me about it and know that he can do that without reprimand, without fear of punishment and shame, is more of a reflection of our relationship. It gave me the opportunity to see that when my sons come to me to admit something they've done wrong and want to make amends for, there's space for us to have an intimate, connected and beautiful conversation.

These moments of witnessing and vulnerability start to build neural pathways in their brains. Now, they will have this knowing: *I can speak to Mum about difficult things, and it will bring us closer together, not further apart.*

I invite you to be aware of these types of conversations. They can be conversations you have with loved ones, or with yourself.

**Ask yourself:**
- Where am I choosing shame when I don't have to?
- Where am I making someone wrong—or myself wrong—as opposed to looking at it as a misstep?

PART 3 - ALLOWING TO BLOOM

# How to make a decision (nine-step process)

Ready? Here's my nine-step process of making a decision in 30 seconds.
- List all your potential options.
- Choose the two options that you're most drawn to.
- Assign heads to one option, and tails to the other.
- Flip a coin.
- That's your answer.
- Did you get that pang of disappointment in your belly? If so, then choose the other option.
- Decide that this decision is the best possible option for you.
- Don't second-guess yourself.
- Proceed like it's already a roaring success.

This is the key to creating momentum in your life and moving you out of the safety of sameness and inertia. We waste a ridiculous amount of energy considering all the options and not moving forward, and then we indulge in indecision, doubt and confusion about which one is 'the best option'.

Here's the thing… what you choose actually doesn't matter. The title of your book, where you're going to go on holiday, whether to stay in or leave the relationship, none of it actually matters. What *does* matter is that you make a decision and act on it. Now, I can guarantee that you're going to have to work a few things out along the way, and there will most definitely be failures, but that doesn't mean it was the wrong decision.

I used this process to decide to shave off my hair, to move to Australia, to run a marathon, to complete my marriage. When we decide and commit, the Universe conspires to move us in that direction. When we doubt ourselves—and constantly consider alternatives—that's when we have split energy. We're saying one thing, but feeling another.

So that thing that you've been going back and forth on…

**Ask yourself:**
- What if I just made the decision, one way or the other, and then moved forwards with complete belief that this is the best thing for me right now?
- How might I show up in my days?
- What might my life look like?
- How might it affect my relationships with the people I love?

PART 3 - ALLOWING TO BLOOM

# Settling in to joy

It's hard to feel joyful amid chaos. The very nature of chaos has us on hyper alertness. If we grew up in a chaotic household, then chaos can feel comforting in its familiarity and, oftentimes, as adults, we unknowingly create this chaos because of the familiarity we have with it. It can see us sabotaging relationships, jobs and environments that are calm and nurturing.

Our brains seek the path of least resistance, and sometimes, that well-trodden path is one of disorganisation and uncertainty. Cultivating order in our lives is an act of immense generosity and kindness. Being able to predict the order of the unfolding of even the most mundane tasks sends a signal to our nervous system that all is well. It allows us to experience the harmony of joy. Joy isn't about structure or organisation, as such. It's about the smooth flow of energy that such order enables.

Where can you weave in a gentle structure today to smooth out the flow of your energy? Maybe it's taking five minutes to sit in solitude when you get in the car to drive to work. Perhaps you take ten minutes to quietly prepare for the weekly meeting with your team. Maybe it's reading five minutes of a book you love before you transition from work mode to home mode. Perhaps it's a five-minute shower by candlelight before bed.

When order is present, joy settles in and invites energy to flow smoothly.

PART 3 - ALLOWING TO BLOOM

# Calling done at B-

Everything I've created and offered to the world has been a solid B- grade. If you identify as a bit of a perfectionist, this will no doubt have you frozen and on the verge of passing out.

All too often, I see people stuck and frustrated because that thing they've been working on—the painting, the course, the book, the business—they believe it's not ready for the world yet. But in truth, it was ready for the world a long time ago. You just didn't give yourself permission to release it and for it to take up space in its imperfection.

I'm not suggesting that we put out sloppy work in the world. What I'm suggesting is that we aim for B-, then release it to the world. Submit the manuscript, show the art, offer the program, launch the business.

Let's look at it from another angle. The fact that you have something that's at a B- means that you've already gone through the hardest part of the process: starting! Waiting until you achieve an A+ most likely means that this piece of work will never be seen by another pair of eyes. It'll remain on your laptop, in the cupboard, in a Google Drive folder or hidden in the back of the storage unit. You can always refine and improve, but you have to give your work an opportunity to be received first.

It can be tricky to know when to call done on a project. As we continue to learn, grow and gain more insight from our experiences, it can feel like we've got more to add, that we can make our thing better. This is true. (As I write these words in my first book, I'm living this experience in real time!) What I suggest is when you've reached your B-, gift this to the world and then get back to work, either on the next iteration of your work or on something fresh and new.

B- projects have the ability to heal, to teach, to support, to improve people's lives and to make the world a more beautiful place. It's you who needs it to be A+, not the world or the people waiting for that very thing to exist. So dust it off, get it to B- and then release it to the world.

PART 3 - ALLOWING TO BLOOM

# Worry

Worry presents itself to the world as loving compassion, but it's a pitiful martyr in disguise. We can feel powerless to worry, but we *always* have the option of whether it's an active part of our experience. We tend to believe that the events of our lives are what's causing us to feel worried. But how we choose to interpret the situations—the thoughts we're having about the circumstances we face—is what's actually causing the worry.

Worry is an interesting emotion because, often, it's not even about us. We worry about what someone else in our life is doing or not doing. We make their actions and decisions a source of worry for us. What's most likely happening here is that we're distracting ourselves from things in our own life. We're using all our brain power and energy to focus on our concern for what someone else is doing or not doing. What's fascinating is that worrying about someone else doesn't help them at all, it only causes discomfort within us.

It can feel kind and loving, but it's not serving you or them to indulge in worry, and the majority of what we choose to worry about will never eventuate. It's like we're suffering about the potential future, not what's actually happening. As the Stoic philosopher Seneca said, 'We suffer more in imagination than in reality.'

So, where today can you lay down the worry and direct that energy to something more worthy of your love and attention?

PART 3 - ALLOWING TO BLOOM

# Living with myself

Half of the time I live with my two sons. The other half of the time I live alone. The first time I ever lived alone was in my early 30s. It was a conscious choice; I wanted to live alone. I wanted to get to know myself more and experience a more internally driven life. I'd ticked a lot of boxes—I'd been married, became a parent, bought and sold houses, built a business—and it looked good on the outside. But it left me feeling empty and shallow on the inside.

Even though it'd been a choice, living alone took some getting used to. Those hours between 5pm and 8pm seemed endless without dinners to prepare, baths to run, homework to check and bedtime stories to read. Gradually, over the years, I got used to the aloneness. Living *by* myself felt normal. But recently, I no longer wanted to live *by* myself, I want to create a life *with* myself. Living by myself inferred that there was someone or something missing. I want to be a woman who lived *with* herself, not *by* herself—a woman who was full, content and whole *with* herself, who had companionship, support and love *with* herself.

It was the difference between enjoying the nurturing quality of chosen solitude, and filling the space with distraction to endure loneliness. Living *with* myself prompts me to ask myself what I need and want. It views this time as an invitation to connect, deepen, enjoy and be more present in this beautiful life I get to live. Regardless of your current circumstance, I encourage you to find time to live *with* yourself. Whether that's for an hour, a day, a year or a lifetime.

As author Stephanie Dowrick says, 'How we feel about our own self, how well or little we know our own self, whether we feel alive inside, largely determines the quality of the time we spend alone, as well as the quality of the relationships we have with other people.'

PART 3 - ALLOWING TO BLOOM

# Adding more 'ish to your life

Not everything—in fact, very few things—is required to be done perfectly. We can allow ourselves to be much less concerned about precision than we'd have ourselves believe.

One of my mentor clients had a business idea that'd been living on their hard drive for two years and had never been launched. Everything had to be perfected before they could launch: perfect website, perfect copy, perfect headshots, even the perfect moon phase. This striving for perfection stifles creativity and puts the handbrake on momentum.

A few years ago, I started applying the 'ish factor to everything as a way to curb perfectionism. For example:

- **My house was tidy'ish**—clothes were hung up, the dishwasher was on at night, I had a clear kitchen table.
- **My exercise routine was consistent'ish**—I'd work out three to five times a week and walk the dog most days.
- **My eating habits were clean'ish**—I ate simple meals with some sort of veggies during the week and we enjoyed family pizza night on Fridays.

What I discovered is that adding more 'ish to your life makes things incredibly more fun, allows for the flow of ease and creates vast open spaces for adventure and spontaneity.

**Ask yourself:**
- How can I add more 'ish to my life today?
- What can I care less about?
- What can I be a little more reckless with and a little less constricted by?

PART 3 - ALLOWING TO BLOOM

# Travelling intuitively

*This is the note from Day 50 of my 100 Day Journey:*

Here we are, at the halfway point of our 100 Day Journey together.

Have you embarked on your own 100 Day Journey alongside me?

If so, how are you travelling?

What has faded into the background?

What has come to the fore?

I decided to start this 100 Day Journey to track my own evolution and to see what patterns emerged, what sparks flickered a little more brightly. One of the biggest discoveries I've made is in recognising that I tend to wither and fade in situations where I feel a heavy sense of obligation. I've also realised that to experience the feelings I most want to feel—joy, peace, freedom, connection, intimacy, contribution—I need to expand and be creative in how I invite these feelings into my life.

I can have a tendency to be one-tracked with my desires and to assign particular feelings to certain roles or responsibilities in my life.

For example:
- Connection via kids.
- Intimacy via partner.
- Contribution via work.

I've been playing with melding these areas together. Weaving intimacy into my work, cultivating connection through strangers I meet at the cafe, offering contribution though sharing stories with people and offering support where appropriate.

This has had me say 'yes' to projects and opportunities that I wouldn't have had access to before. This year has shifted a little and the coming months feel fresh, new and beautifully unscripted. In order to create space for these new projects, it's nudged me to simplify my life yet again… which is exactly what this 100 Day Journey was intended for! To expand, allow and align with the new that feels exciting.

What this means is that I'm going to take a side trip on our 100 Day Journey. Like with all intuitive travel, we can start with an itinerary only for it to be thrown out for something we couldn't have planned for before we set off. The structure of our journey together will be a little different during this second half. Emails will be less frequent—think of them as little postcards from my travels.

PART 3 - ALLOWING TO BLOOM

**What I've learned:**
- We get to decide what our journey looks like.
- We get to change our minds and our hearts.
- We get to follow what feels exciting.

This isn't about ticking days off on the calendar. It's about carving out some space to settle into and feel into our next right step. Our journeys are far richer when we take the time to stop and look around, and detours are always, always guiding us to more of what we want.

# Reflections and Final Thoughts

    This point of the journey can feel, in a lot of ways, like we're approaching the final destination. There are people, opportunities, experiences and ways of being coming into our reality that previously were barely a whisper of an idea. But calling done at this stage of the journey will not leave us satisfied for long.

    Our nature as humans is to always be in the process of becoming. We achieve something, then we've got our eye on the next prize that's not quite visible yet. We have a tendency to use this as a reason to beat ourselves up, to shame ourselves for never being happy with what we have, for always being in the energy of longing for more.

    If you find yourself here, let me reassure you that nothing has gone wrong. This is just simply part of the natural cycle. The very nature of a cycle is that it's perpetual. It's a process that repeats itself again and again in the same order.

You stand in a new place now than when you embarked on this journey. You have a keener understanding and greater sensitivity about who you are and how you want to proceed. From here, we refine and continue to cycle through this process of tilling the soil, sowing the seeds and allowing to bloom.

Refining our lives is a subtractive process, not an additive one. It's about un-layering, unmasking and un-seducing ourselves from the life we've been conditioned to desire and instead, create one that feels truly liberating and creative. It's about untethering what's good to welcome in what's great. And this untethering asks for the seeds of your courage to be sewn.

The process of compiling these notes into a complete book has allowed me to experience their wisdom and insights in different ways. They have become study prompts for me to use in new situations that have emerged since first writing them.

Over the past few months, a few key messages have bubbled to the surface. They have become guiding nudges of support and encouragement and been incredibly helpful in moments where courage has felt almost elusive. I offer them to you, for your journey ahead.

**The components of this new beginning are already gathered.**

Few things happen without any foreshadowing. It can feel like we're taken by surprise, but it's more often that we've busied ourselves to the point of being unable to see, hear or feel the quiet forming of this new beginning. May you find the stillness and quiet to hear the whispers of your new beginnings.

**It's safe to outgrow who you were to become who you are.**

Change is uncomfortable and awkward. Even when we feel the sense of having outgrown a place, person or situation, there's a period of grieving for what we had hoped and wished for that to become. May you find the gentle strength to trust that you're blooming into gardens that are ready and waiting for you.

**Proceed with small moments of care towards yourself.**

You don't have to force your unfolding and blooming, it's inevitable. It's what naturally wants to occur. May you lay down all heavy doing and striving and feel the magic of grace do your life for you, through you and with you.

**Keep asking, keep giving, keep opening.**

All is well. Everything is in support of you. Deep in your bones and in the newly expanding corners of your heart, you know this to be true. The deck is stacked firmly in your favour. Sometimes, we have to slow down in order to speed up. Focus more on feeling from the heart rather than thinking from the mind. There are infinite possibilities waiting for you. May you recognise the delight and bask in eager anticipation as your seeds of courage take root, sprout, grow and bloom, as you allow all of who you are to emerge in the next of many new beginnings.

# Acknowledgements

I feel so honoured to be surrounded by people who remind me to kindle my courage each and every day.

To my publisher, Natasha - thank you for holding the vision for this book along with me from day one. You're guidance and excitement about these words has been such a gift to me as a writer.

To my editor, Ally - thank you for taking my words and polishing them so beautifully and with such care.

To Gabe, your courage to be all of who you are since the day you were born is the most beautiful thing to witness. You remind me that it's okay to be me by the way you move through the world. Thank you for choosing me to be your mum.

To Noah, you are pure joy embodied. The simple and natural way you see the world, and how you always choose to orient towards the best in every person, is a gift to our family and everyone you meet. You remind me to live with an open heart. I love being on this adventure with you.

To Cassidy, thank you for your love and support as I've gone through the process of bringing this book to life. Your steady love, consistent encouragement and unwavering belief in me and my work has meant more than you know. I love you.

To Lauren, thank you for your excitement and the straight-talking advice you've offered from the other side of the world, especially in the times I needed it most. I love that Dad's love of books flows through us both.

To all of my friends, especially Tash, Caitlin, Cara, Melissa, Elisha, Nicola, Elka, Bess, Greer, EJ, Dixie and Stef. You are all the most courageous women. My life is richer, deeper and more joyful because of my friendship with each of you.

Finally, to all of my clients over the years, thank you for your openness and vulnerability. Being trusted with your stories and witnessing you kindle your courage day after day is an absolute gift.

# About the author

Vari McKechnie is an author, mentor and podcaster. She works with clients who are ready to dial up the joy and contribution in their lives through cultivating more ease and courage.

With more than a decade of experience as a designer, creative director and illustrator, she also works with organisations on how to bring their businesses into greater alignment to create deeper, more meaningful connections with their clients and customers.

On her podcast, 'The Vari McKechnie Podcast', she shares insights and lessons learned in the art of living well.

Originally from Glasgow, Scotland, Vari has called Australia home since 2007. She currently lives on the Mornington Peninsula, just outside of Melbourne with her two sons, Gabe and Noah and their adorable dog, Stella.

- Find out more about how to work with Vari on her website: varimckechnie.com
- Follow Vari on Instagram: @varimckechnie
- Search 'The Vari McKechnie Podcast' wherever you get your podcasts.

Milton Keynes UK
Ingram Content Group UK Ltd.
UKHW040636301023
431584UK00004B/369